Howard. Shirley Cartier

Mrs Shirley Cartier
2475 Holford Rd RR 4
Mill Bay BC V0R 2P4

FLYNN'S COVE

FLYNN'S COVE

Bethine Flynn

Illustrated by Chris Buffett

Porthole Press Ltd.
Sidney, British Columbia
1986

Cover by Chris Buffett

Published by Porthole Press Ltd.
2082 Neptune Road
Sidney, B.C. V8L 3X9

Text set by The Typeworks
Printed in Canada

Canadian Cataloguing in Publication Data

Flynn, Bethine
    Flynn's cove
ISBN 0-919931-10-3
    1. Flynn, Bethine 2. Vancouver Island (B.C.)—
Biography. I. Title.

    FC3844. 3.F59A3 1986 971.1'34 C86-090094-0
    F1089.V3F59 1986

I dedicate Flynn's Cove with much affection to my daughter Maureen Pinton and my teacher Zola Helen Ross.

Contents

Prologue		9
1.	The Cove	12
2.	Nuchatlitz	17
3.	Almost an Indian	24
4.	Return of the *Pigeon*	35
5.	The Gift	44
6.	Nit Picking	51
7.	Christie Celebrations	58
8.	Arrival of the Grandchildren	64
9.	A Menacing Visitor	73
10.	On Patrol	83
11.	Epidemic	94
12.	Loss of a Friend	106
13.	Cedar Bark Craft	115
14.	AA's at Ahouset	124
15.	Sophie's Surprise	133
16.	'The Boat Sank'	138
17.	'Sophie Come Home in a Box'	145
18.	'No Damn Room for Ladies'	155
19.	Chief Dan at Christie	170
20.	Wedding	178
21.	Disaster and Recovery	183
Epilogue		191

Prologue

I knew our aircraft was in a dive. I knew our altitude, a mere four hundred feet, allowed Wally only seconds for maneuvering, yet I felt no fear. I was, in truth, strangely detached. If we missed those reefs that stood like sentinels in the path of our seaplane, we would be all right. And then we hit, bouncing a good fifty feet back into the skies. We hit again. We hit again. This time we stayed down and I realized, belatedly, were it not for fate we could well have been sitting far beneath those waters that poured into Esperanza Inlet from the Pacific Ocean just two miles to the west.

Wally flung open his door and eased himself down onto the pontoon. In a few minutes he called up to me. "She's okay. No broken struts. Darn sturdy plane, this *Pigeon* of ours."

Now, with Wally out on the pontoon checking for damage, I began a more personal examination. Something warm was trickling down my chin. I swiped at it with the back of my hand. Blood. The front of my blouse was also stained red. And then I remembered.... Wally hauling back on the wheel, attempting to pull us out of the dive, then the impact. My mouth had struck the wheel on my side of the plane. I felt no pain, but when I explored to find the source of the blood, I found the inside my mouth was cut and my teeth wiggled ever so slightly.

"Darn, if I've wrecked my teeth!" My anger was like a flash of lightning. It came and it went, and I laughed to myself. Such flashes of anger had brought me through the many crises encountered in our flying veterinary practice from our hospital in Seattle, up the coast of British Columbia as far north as Sitka in southeastern Alaska. The anger had countered both fear and hysteria. It had eased the exasperating distractions we had encountered in establishing a home on our 116 acre Nootka Island estate, as rugged and isolated an area as could be found. Our nearest neighbours were the Indians at the village of Nuchatlitz, four sea-miles distant. There were no roads, no trails. Our only contact with the outside world was our seaplane, our yellow *Pigeon.*

The least I could do now was join Wally in signalling a troller he had spotted in the distance. Assured by its steady approach that the troller's pilot had seen our signal, we both climbed back into the cabin. For the first time, Wally saw my mouth. His reaction was a combination of dismay and disbelief.

"How in the world did you manage to do that?"

"It was easy!" I replied ruefully.

Any strain that might have lingered between us was effectively defused. This incident was only one of many that could have forced us back to a more conventional life-style had it not been for a deep love for our wilderness home, and an innate ability to counter hardships and adversities with humour.

Wally had a fatal heart attack on September 5th, 1960. After the initial shock, I was able to summon the needed ingredients to sustain me in this tragedy.

"How could you go and leave me alone?" I had cried out in desperation and anger. "How could you?"

But in the months that followed my love for our island home surmounted all other feelings. The old log house and the cove had comforted me, had given me purpose and direction. I loved it all . . . the semi-circular cove framed by towering evergreens, its pellucid waters protected from the rougher waters of Esperanza Inlet by three rocky islets. Across the cove, opposite my old log house, stood the charming little English cottage that had come with the purchase of an additional 112 acres. There hadn't been time to make the cottage livable, but I visited it often, wandering through its three small rooms, climbing the cement steps up the bluff at the back of the house. No one, I thought, could want for anything more.

CHAPTER 1

The Cove

S ummer, 1964. No matter the musty smells in my old log house when first I'd arrived at my hidden cove. No matter the mouse droppings that had to be brushed from a chair before I could sit down. A log cabin depressing? Not to me, though I recalled how unnerved I'd been when Wally and I, back in 1956, had first entered this house.

I'd thrilled to the cove the moment we glimpsed it from our seaplane as we circled for a landing. I'd even been impressed with the house, perched on a thirty foot bluff, encircled by the forest—until I saw the kitchen. Never, I'd protested, could I function here. Horrid brown walls, windows smothered by brush no one had bothered to cut back.

I could laugh now, thinking back on that time.

A May-day sun smiled through my windows, glimmering peek-a-boo shafts filtering through the new greenness of my filbert trees. How they'd grown, their branches reaching out to caress the old house! The soft scraping sound as swaying branches rubbed against the hardness of log walls was pleasing to my ears, a restful, relaxing sound, harmonizing with my mood. I felt no urgency to get things done. The whole summer stretched out before me offering its most precious gift . . . time.

I wandered from room to room, gloating. The kitchen, which Wally had painted all pink and white, no longer depressed me. The huge wood-burning cookstove was a guarantee of warmth and hot meals. I entered the living room—apple-green log walls, cedar log beams. Resisting the appeal of a pink upholstered rocker, I peeked into the rooms on either side of the living room, then climbed the stairs to check the three upstairs bedrooms. Their cedar-paneled walls and secret closets still intrigued and delighted me.

The sun beckoned me through the upstairs windows. I loved the old house.

But the out-of-doors . . . that was the glory. I ran from the house and down the steps to the beach. I always ran down those steps, though more than one visitor had suggested that doing so invited disaster. There was a freedom, an exhilaration, in taking those steps at breakneck speed, a defiance of the measured caution of a more cultured world. I leapt the last two steps, landing lightly on the rocky beach.

I stopped then, as I always did, to survey my kingdom. Flynn's Cove, we had christened it, and the name had held. As I looked out across Esperanza Inlet to the forested mountains that lined the inlet, I recalled the words of a visitor that first summer I was alone here.

"This is no place for a woman," he'd said. "It's too isolated, too lonely. No telephone, not even a radio-phone. What if you get sick or hurt?"

I'd laughed at his fears and he joined in, then added, "Okay, laugh now, Bethine Flynn, but I give you three years. Mark my word, you'll have a bellyful of it by then!"

And I laughed now, spontaneously, joyfully responding to the wind whispering through the filbert leaves and the faint rustlings in the bushes, reminding me of the many forest creatures sharing my domain. Three years had come and gone since Wally died and, if it were possible, I loved this place more now than I did then.

"If ever I leave here it will be because of some radical happening over which I have no control."

I'd spoken aloud. The words sobered me for a moment. Impatiently, I pushed the thought aside, and then forgot it completely as my noisy seagulls, Reuben and Rachel, swooped in for a landing only yards from where I stood. They regarded me tentatively, taking a few calculated steps in my direction.

"Sorry, kids, no treats today. You'll have to rustle your own."

Actually, I seldom tossed tidbits their way. They were obstreperous enough without any encouragement from me. But pushy as they were, I enjoyed their company. Other gulls came and went, but these two were always somewhere about. I could never feel lonely with Reuben and Rachel screaming defiance, or maybe a welcome, every time I trespassed on *their* beach.

Shrill squeals diverted my attention. Beady eyes peered out from the bush that converged on the beach. My mink, Jasper and Tessie, would soon be playing, once they had determined it was really me on their beach and not some inquisitive stranger. Jasper had allowed me, during my first summer here alone, to treat an ugly wound above his tail. Tessie had paraded her young right by me as I sat on a boulder. They were special, these two.

I saw a boat approaching. It was Pat Little, an Indian neighbour from Nuchatlitz. Pat was a young man, taller than most of his people. He pulled his boat in close, then leapt for shore. "Hi," he said as he looped his anchor rope around a boulder. "You want some wood cut, Mrs. Flynn?"

"I can't refuse an offer like that, Pat. The day is too beautiful. I just want to sit here and do nothing."

"Days always beautiful," Pat replied with a grin. "You sit. I'll cut wood."

"How did you know I was here?"

"I was to Esperanza. Alf say he and Cathy bring you out.... I'll get your axe, Mrs. Flynn."

Pat had helped me before. I didn't need to show him where the axe was. Left to myself, my thoughts turned to Cathy and Alf and my trip up from Seattle where I stayed a part of each winter to be near my daughter, Maureen.

Cathy and Alf, two summers ago, had spent the first day of their honeymoon here at my cove—the most beautiful place they could think of for a honeymoon, they told me. They worked at the small mission hospital at Esperanza; Cathy as a nurse, Alf as maintenance man. They had little free time, but what little they had they spent at the cove....

Somewhere in the back of my mind I could hear the thud, thud, thud, as Pat swung the axe into rolls of fir. I'd day-dreamed too long. If I didn't hurry there'd be no coffee or sandwich for Pat when he decided to quit. He nodded and grinned as I raced past him and up the steps.

Pat soon joined me up the house. "Rose wants you to come to Nuchatlitz," he said. "She will tell Father Larkin next time he comes."

I struggled to hide a grin. It was Father Larkin's nature to do the telling. As far as I knew, Rose was the only one who dared tell him anything. Whatever she told him, he did, and with a certain amused satisfaction. I had written him I was coming but most likely he hadn't seen my letter yet. As parish priest, he was often away from his base at Tahsis, visiting Indian villages as far as Kyuquot, about thirty miles to the north of me.

Pat finished his sandwich and I ran ahead of him down to the beach, where it was my habit to bid my guests good-bye.

"See you soon," he said.

I sat on a boulder watching him maneuver his boat through the reefs that partially blocked the entrance to my cove, and I thought of Rose. She and I had been best friends from our first meeting. Her father-in-law, Felix Michael, had been Chief of Nuchatlitz then. Now his son Alban, her husband, was Chief. Never, I reflected, could I wish for better friends and neighbors than the people of Nuchatlitz. Already, through Pat, I'd been welcomed home.

CHAPTER 2

Nuchatlitz

No question! Those were Minniebelle's feet clicking the full length of my kitchen roof. It was a demand for me to join her.

"I know," I said as I stepped through the door. "It's too nice a day to be inside, but I do have to eat."

The grouse regarded me from her favorite perch in the plum tree that grazed the north wall of the kitchen. We'd never enjoyed plums from that tree. The green plums that did appear, Minniebelle delighted in dropping at me. I'd never been able to decide whether it was a game or merely an attention-getter.

My eyes strayed from Minniebelle to take in the clutter of planks and boards Wally and I had tossed aside when we tore a rickety old porch off the front of the house.

"If I'm really serious about coming up here summer after summer," I confided to Minniebelle, "I should do something with those darn boards." And she nodded her head. "I could stack them in the garden area, seeing as I don't have a garden anyway."

Did I catch a disapproving glint in Minniebelle's eyes? Wally hadn't minded that she and her progeny took far more than their share from our garden, but I was neither so ambitious, nor so generous.

"Out of sight, out of mind," I remembered my mother saying as she stashed a box of treasures she couldn't use—yet didn't want to give up—into a dark corner in the closet. I found my corner down on the first level. Shoved in amongst sword ferns which grew to half my height, the boards should be sufficiently camouflaged.

For one my build (five foot two, an approximate hundred pounds) it would take weeks to complete the project, but I had plenty of time.

Father Larkin came in one day and caught me at my task. "Whatever in the world are you up to?" he asked.

"Seems pretty obvious to me," I replied. "I'm getting rid of the boards cluttering up my yard."

His deep belly laugh was discomfiting. "It's obvious you do things the hard way," he said. "Did you ever think of sliding them down the steps?" And as I shook my head, "At least you could have found a more accessible hiding place. You're running an obstacle course."

"Oh, I'm careful," I assured him.

"Maybe," he conceded, then added, "How are the new shingles working out? I hear the Birtles did the job for you before you left last summer."

"Yes, Cathy and Alf to the rescue. As you said, the Lord provided. As to how they're working out, well, it hasn't rained yet."

"It will!"

"I'm sure." But when I asked if the adding machine I'd given him in exchange had really paid for all those shingles, he merely nodded, focusing his attention on the boards.

"Women!" he muttered, shaking his head. "Always have to be moving something around. Don't expect me to help you. It's all I can do to carry my own weight up those steps. But carry on. You'll get the job done... someday!" Before I could reply he'd changed the subject.

"Rose tells me you're coming to Nuchatlitz. We'd best get a move on."

I stifled a laugh. "Could I wash first, and change into a dress?"

"I suppose you must. Well, hurry it up."

We were soon on our way, rounding the curve of Nootka Island, winding our way through smaller outer islands, dodging reefs. Father Larkin piloted his boat with a certain flourish, almost a disdain of those reefs, yet to my knowledge he'd never struck one. His cavalier attitude was contagious and my spirits soared. I laughed aloud as we swerved abruptly, and I saw waves rippling over the reefs we'd missed. Our fantailed spray washed the air with the tangy smell of the sea, and the breeze that accompanied us carried its own delicate blending of sea and forest perfumes. How fortunate I was to live in an area where one must travel by boat!

We flashed by the fish camp so fast I couldn't tell if either Cecily or Bruce was on deck. The fish camp—anchored in waters sheltered by several islands—sat like a sitting duck, its long dock trailing out behind. There were no boats anchored alongside. The men were out fishing. Cecily and Bruce worked the camp, earning money for Bruce's college education. At the end of the season the entire camp would be towed to a winter moorage.

Like a lovely etching, frame houses crouched along the shore. Nuchatlitz, secure on its own small island. There were no trollers anchored alongside their floating dock either, but our boat had been spotted. Running figures traversed the stretch of green grass kept cropped by Nuchatlitz' free-roaming cattle. Several small children reached the dock before we did, grasping our boat. The older children would still be in school at Christie, some seventy miles down coast.

"Bethine!" Rose greeted me, "I knew it would be you.

Hi, Father Larkin. You just caught me. I was going for water."

"Your pump break down again?" he asked.

She shrugged, then giggled. Laughter came easily to Rose. "I guess," she said. "But I have water. I can make coffee."

I stepped onto the dock. Rose took me in her arms and gently kissed my cheek; a salutation I returned.

Father Larkin observed, "Anyone would think you two hadn't seen each other in months."

"As if we had," I said. And I laughed out of sheer happiness. It was good to be at Nuchatlitz again.

With youngsters tugging at our arms we made our way up to the house. Rose's house was nearest the dock but I saw Evelyn Little and Julie Smith standing in their doorways and waved. They hadn't come to the dock, knowing that I always visited with Rose first.

"Could I help you get water?" I asked as she set the coffee on to perk.

"No, Evelyn will come. Not room in the boat for more. Too many buckets."

"I won't offer," Father Larkin put in. "I'd sink your boat."

"Yes, Father," Rose agreed. "I think so." And the dark brown eyes smiled.

It had seemed strange to me when first we'd moved to the island that one could be surrounded by water, in an area of predominately heavy rains, and still have a water shortage. I was more fortunate than my neighbors, for three small streams cascaded down my bluffs and into the cove. But I, too, had experienced water shortages when the hot summer sun reduced my streams to a trickle. Here at Nuchatlitz the problem was even more acute. There were no streams on their flat little island. Their water supply was a small lake on Nootka Island.

To Rose, it was just one of those things. Father Larkin and I sat sipping our coffee, watching as Rose and Evelyn rowed out in their boat.

"Do you think I'll ever be as unruffled and accepting as Rose?" I asked him.

"No," he said.

I wrinkled my nose at him and changed the subject. "Are we going to have Mass?"

"Yes, in one hour. That should give Rose time enough."

"Good. I'll finish this coffee and run down to the Saveys."

Nuchatlitz was like one big family, I reflected, all age groups working together, helping each other. Wilson, Pat's father, was about my age. Rose was younger than I, but not by too many years. The Saveys, and Felix and Lily Michael, were the oldest members, the grandparents, loved and respected by all.

Frank and Sophie met me at the door. "We know you will come to see us," Frank said, and Sophie nodded a smiling agreement. Sophie spoke no English, but she had a feeling for what was said.

When the Saveys and the Michaels were young it had not been thought too important for girls to attend school. That they could not speak English was still not considered a handicap. Life had been their teacher, and when they spoke, everyone listened. They were the knowledgeable ones, sought out when decisions affecting all must be made.

Sophie must have been beautiful when she was young. Now in her seventies, she was a lovely lady. Her bobbed white hair framed her face like a cap. Her chocolate brown eyes reflected an inner happiness which bubbled to the surface in her smile. In Frank's eyes I saw the same inner composure. Two happy people.

Inside the house there was a babel of voices. Evelyn's
children had converged on the Saveys when Evelyn went
for water with Rose. Rose's little ones had tagged along.
There were probably others. I couldn't identify them all.
It didn't matter to Frank and Sophie that only Evelyn's
children were really their grandchildren. They loved
them all.

Anticipating my visit, coffee and peanut butter and
jelly sandwiches had been prepared in advance. The
Savey's house had no view of the dock, but one of the
children would have carried the news of my arrival.

We lingered over coffee and sandwiches until Evelyn
arrived, lugging an oversize pail of water. She shooed the
children out.

"Go home. Get dressed for Mass."

Sophie disappeared into the bedroom to put on her
best dress and I left with Evelyn, stopping only a moment
at her house, then continuing on alone to Rose's. I didn't
knock at her door. I just walked in, as much at home
there as in my own house. Rose heard me and called from
a bedroom.

I'm dressed in a minute. Have to hurry. Father Larkin
don't like it to be late."

"I know," I said, but secretly I doubted he was as impatient as he was purported to be. At the cove, delight-
fully lackadaisical, I adhered to Indian time, paying heed
only to the tides and the setting sun, and not always to
them. Father Larkin, knowing how lax we all were, used
impatience as a tool. When the church bell rang, we were
ready.

"Rose, you are beautiful," I said as we walked towards the church, the little ones running beside us.

She smiled, pleased. Her long dark hair, pulled back in
a pony-tail, accentuated the gentle roundness of her
cheeks and her delicate features. The white sweater she

wore over her dress enhanced the lovely color of her smooth skin. I recalled mama saying to me, "Don't frown. Frowns make wrinkles." *Rose will never have wrinkles*, I thought. Even when troubled, I had never seen her frown.

The walk to the church was a colourful parade, everyone dressed in their Sunday best, though Sunday it was not. Rose and I walked slowly, pausing often so that I might speak to friends I hadn't seen in many months. The church, a white frame building with a prominent bell tower, resembled any one of the small churches that had been built in all areas of the country at the turn of the century—churches now termed picturesque. To me they seem more churchly in appearance than their more modern counterparts. The church sat well back of the houses and off to the side. In the background, Pacific waters washed the sandy beach and reflected the blue of a cloudless sky. Beautiful, and tranquil beyond words, it put me in a receptive frame of mind to enter the church.

After Mass, as we strolled back to Rose's house, stopping now and again to exchange greetings, I mentioned Father Larkin would probably want to be leaving right away.

"You don't leave now," Rose said. "We will eat first. I will tell Father. I have a salmon Alban caught and I bake bread this morning. When you go, I will give you a loaf."

It was a sumptuous meal, and Father's comment, as we headed back over the waters, was telling.

"The more impatient I am, the better I fare." And he grinned.

CHAPTER 3

Almost an Indian

I worked hard those days after my visit to Nuchatlitz, determined to get the clutter out of my yard. Possibly, also, there was a streak of stubbornness in my make-up. When Father Larkin came again he'd see that when a woman makes up her mind to do something it's as good as done. I was encouraged as the stack among the ferns kept growing and the clutter in the yard no longer resembled a clutter.

There was one four-by-six, much heavier than the boards and at least twelve feet long. I avoided looking at it—out of sight, out of mind—but the day came when I could avoid it no longer. It was all that was left to move.

"Softy!" I berated myself. "Look at your muscles. You can carry it!"

It was even heavier than I had anticipated, but once I had it up in my arms, pride forestalled any idea of putting it down. I staggered to the top of the steps, fumbled for the first step, and missed. In a sitting position I bumped all the way to the bottom, the four-by-six seeming to propel me along. I clung to it, not knowing what else to do with it.

At the bottom, still in a sitting position, still clutching the four-by-six, my foot slammed into the immovable cast-iron wheel of a cart I used to pack wood to the foot of the steps. Pain surged up my leg and into the topmost reaches of my head. I bit my lip to hold back a cry and squeezed my eyes tight shut, but I couldn't shut out the pain. How could just a toe hurt so much?

How long I sat there, eyes closed, my head tipped back, I couldn't be sure. No thoughts found their way through the density of the pain. But finally I shook my head and opened my eyes. I realized I was still cradling that four-by-six, and that my toe was still wedged up against the wheel. With an effort I put the plank aside and pulled my foot up to stare woefully at a swollen and discolored member.

"Darn!" I muttered between clenched teeth. "And I wasn't even running."

I stood on one foot, looking at those steps. It had never seemed such a long way up. I made it, a step at a time, but a couple of days later when Slim Beale came in on his weekly run from Zeballos with my groceries, I was still hobbling around.

"What happened to you?" he demanded.

"Broke my toe, I guess." And I told him how it happened.

Slim had been bringing my groceries and supplies ever since I'd been alone at the cove. Kindness was an integral part of his make-up. On more than one occasion he'd helped me with jobs I couldn't handle alone. But today he wasted no sympathy on me.

"Why don't you get help for jobs like that? There are plenty of men in this country who'd jump at the chance to help out."

"Maybe, but I wanted to do it myself."

"Well, now that you've banged yourself up, I hope you've decided to go easy."

The weather forced me to take it easy for a few days.

The skies opened up and the rain poured down. The snap and crackle of a wood fire kept the house cozy and warm and the new shingles were a decided improvement over the pots and pans I'd formerly been forced to set out to catch the leaks. It was nice not having to dodge raindrops as I prepared my meals and washed dishes.

When I dashed out to the woodshed for wood to refill the woodbox, I saw that my rain barrels were filling. Like my Indian neighbors, I welcomed this supply that fell free from the skies.

With the sun came the McLeans from their mission establishment at Esperanza. Dr. McLean was the missionary doctor. It was from him we had purchased the little cottage across the cove. I jokingly upbraided him for not having come when my toe was giving me trouble.

"Didn't you get my message?" I teased him. "I thought you'd be receptive to mental telepathy."

He laughed. "From now on," he assured me, "I'll pay more attention when messages like that come my way. I presume it's okay now. You haven't even asked me to look at it."

"Doesn't hurt at all," I admitted.

Somehow time got away from us that day. The McLeans were caught on the low tide and forced to spend the night. They didn't mind.

"It's so peaceful here," the doctor said. There was a wistful note in his voice and I realized that lack of time to enjoy the cottage had been a determining factor in persuading him to give it up.

A few days after the McLeans' visit I saw a troller approaching the cove. Instead of coming in, however, it inched up to a ledge on my outer beach. A head poked out the pilot's window and a shout ruptured the morning stillness.

"Hello, Mrs. Flynn!"

Moses Smith was Rose's father. He never exhibited any of the shyness or reticence that seemed to be a part of Indian make-up. With Indian or white man, he was equally at ease. He could, and would, expound on any subject. He was also an inveterate tease, with an unfailing sense of humour. What could he be doing? Certainly he hadn't come for a visit or he would have come into the cove.

His baffling maneuver lent wings to my feet. I bounded over the rocks, leaping from boulder to boulder. Moses was laughing.

"It's okay, Mrs. Flynn," he said. "We'll wait. We go to Zeballos. You like to come?"

"Sure would."

A quick glance had taken in the Saveys sitting out on deck, and Martha Amos appeared from the pilot house. She and Moses pulled me aboard. Moses and Martha lived at Queens Cove. Undoubtedly they had gone to Nuchatlitz to see Rose and had taken the Saveys aboard. Indians seldom travel with an empty boat.

"Now you are almost an Indian," Frank told me with a broad grin. "You run good." He moved over, making room for me to sit between him and Sophie.

I hadn't been to Zeballos since Wally's death. I found the town unchanged. We walked the dusty road from the long dock up to town, past the post office, the hardware store, Slim's home, then the grocery store that took care of my weekly orders. Slim wasn't home. His boat hadn't been at the dock. People and dogs wandered down the middle of the street. No one was in a hurry.

Zeballos is the oldest town in the area, established before Esperanza, before Tahsis, but after the establishment of a store and post office by the Newtons, the original owners of my cove. My old log house, built in 1914, was the first house in the area built by a white man. I was grateful to the Newtons for having the foresight and the courage to persevere in such a rugged and isolated area.

Gold, found in the mountains back of Zeballos, had brought settlers and adventure seekers to the area. In its heyday, Zeballos had boasted a population of two thousand. Now there were probably not even two hundred people to walk the street that stretched no more than a mile or so up the valley.

Moses and Martha and the Saveys stopped at the store. "I'll stop on my way back," I told them.

There was nothing I needed at the store. No sense duplicating the order Slim would be bringing out. I wanted to see the people, many of whose pets we had treated when Wally was alive, and some of whom still sought my advice. As I passed the houses, people waved or came out to say hello. They didn't invite me in, knowing there were many I would want to see in the short time allotted me. It had taken an hour and a half to reach Zeballos. With the tide and the wind against us, the trip home could well take longer and Moses would not want to put me off on the rocks in the dark.

I stopped in at the cafe for a quick cup of coffee, knowing some of the villagers would be gathered here. Later I strolled on up the street, pausing in front of the two-storey frame hotel. I knew the hotel well, having stayed there on a number of occasions. A pub dominated most of the downstairs area. The upstairs rooms, twelve or so, were not insulated against the raucous laughter that filtered up from the pub. Sleeping could be a chancy affair.

My eyes strayed to the firehouse across the street, more generally used as a community hall where old movies were shown. I smiled, recalling the time I'd attended one. It was a social affair. Everyone brought snacks. The benches were hard. Reels had to be changed.

There were breaks in the film. West-coasters, however, are not much inclined to impatience. The hum of voices filled the room. The villagers enjoyed.

I walked as far as the bakery, then turned and walked back to the store. A village store is an experience. The variety of items in that one small room was unparalleled. There were the grocery and meat departments, of course, but somehow room had also been made for many items found in city department stores—clothing, kitchenware, linens, bedding, jewelry, cosmetics, and even a display of basket work brought in by the Indian people.

I spoke to the Wittons who'd owned and operated the store for as long as I'd been in the area, and probably much longer. And I spotted the Saveys. Frank had found a box to sit on. He tired easily.

"Moses and Martha be back in a few minutes," he said. "Is time to go home."

Again I sat on the deck between Frank and Sophie. The wind whipped my hair. There was a chill to that wind, but snugged in a jacket Martha loaned me, I hardly felt it, nor did I mind the silvery spray when we cut into the chop. Moses edged up to the same ledge where he'd picked me up. He lowered me over the side and there I stood, waving, until the troller rounded the islands and I could no longer see it. I turned then and ran back along the beach and up the steps. A fire had to be rebuilt, and I was hungry, oh so hungry.

Minniebelle met me at the top of the steps. The impatient nod of her head and the way she stomped down the path ahead of me showed her displeasure. I'd been gone most of the day and hadn't even told her I was leaving.

"Sorry, Minniebelle, there wasn't time." And then I grinned. No matter her mood, it was nice to have Minniebelle to come home to.

For a long time, after that trip to Zeballos, I didn't have many visitors. Father Larkin roared in from time to time to make sure I was alive and well. And then there was Slim, with his weekly trips with supplies. So May melted into June and June sloshed into July.

I didn't mind the rains. They filled my streams and kept the water flowing through the long plastic hose that brought water into my house. I loved the beat of raindrops on the roof, loved the sizzle of a downpour swishing through the trees. I drank in the freshness as I walked the beach, my shoes squishing with every step. They were wading shoes, meant to get wet. The wet brush stroked my bare legs as I walked my paths. I wore shorts. Wet pants clinging to my legs I didn't like. Every day it rained I bailed my boat, not minding the trickle of rain that ran down my neck. A warm fire in the stove would soon dry me out.

But, oh, the glory of a July sun! Flowers lifted their heads. Trees shook the remaining rain droplets from their branches, sending them cascading upon my head. Hummingbirds darted past my ears, emitting their raucous call, so prodigious a sound from so tiny a body. Frogs croaked in the tall grass. Birds sang, and I sang with them. Minniebelle emerged from the bushes and joined me for a walk down a path into the forest. Squirrels skittered through the trees ahead of us, keeping up an incessant chattering. Their chook, chook, chook reminded me of chickens scratching for food, the sound so similar. My world, indeed, had come alive.

Later in the day, when the tide was low, I checked my beaches. The pungent odor of clams, mussels, crabs, snails, was not offensive. They were a part of my world. Towards evening, when the wind died down, I rowed out from my cove, my body reacting to the motion of the sea, to the rise and fall of ocean swells, gentled by the quiet of late afternoon. At night, too, I rowed out, but only around my islands, for then the landscape blends into the night, confounding the unwary.

One night held an almost ethereal stillness. Not a whisper of the wind, not even a sigh from the sea, no sound from my birds or my animals who had sought the deep bush. I drifted, dipping my oars silently, to keep me on course, reluctant to disturb the stillness that pervaded the night. Above me billions of stars of unbelievable brightness pricked the blackness of the night, their beauty reflecting in the waters of the inlet. As I rowed slowly back towards home a full golden moon rose over the tops of the trees at the south end of the cove. I stopped rowing to watch its majestic ascent into the night sky. I was filled with a quiet exhilaration, totally unlike what I experienced when I pitted my strength against the chop of the sea. This feeling was wondrous, consuming. As in a trance, I followed a moonlit path into the cove. But I couldn't go up to the house, couldn't yet give up the night. So I rowed out once again, and again drifted in on my moonlit path. The moon was not much higher in the sky. Still immersed in the beauty and the peace of the night, I anchored my boat and climbed the steps, pausing often to look up, to marvel, to wonder.

******

Was that voices I'd heard? I'd slept so soundly after my moonlight row. Now the sun was pouring through my bedroom window. I blinked from its brightness and pulled the blankets partially over my head to allow my eyes to adjust. The voice came again.

"Mrs. Flynn, it's only us."

That was Cathy's voice. It jerked me to a sitting position from which I stared at Cathy and Alf, standing just a few feet from my bed. They were laughing.

"I wouldn't believe anyone could sleep like that," Alf said. "We banged on the kitchen door and called your name. No answer. Couldn't figure where you'd gotten to. Decided we'd better check further so we came in and called from the foot of the stairs. Still no answer. The house was so quiet. It was like no one was here."

Cathy took up the tale. "Alf thought we ought to leave, but I figured since we'd come this far we might as well check upstairs. Your bedroom door was open, but then I guess you never close it. Anyway, we called again. You didn't even turn over. If I could sleep like that!"

I joined in their laughter. "I do sleep like a log here," I admitted. "No worries, nothing to disturb me unless the rains come pounding on my roof, or the mice start playing around. Actually, I've gotten used to those sounds as well. I just sleep away."

"You're telling us," Cathy said with a giggle, "but now that we've gotten you awake, do you mind if we go downstairs and build a fire and start breakfast?"

"It will be my pleasure," I assured them. "Help yourself to anything you can find."

They could only stay a couple of hours, but much was accomplished in the allotted time. Cathy, over my protests, washed windows.

"Makes me feel I belong here," she insisted.

Alf was somewhere on the first landing. I could hear the ping of the axe. I managed barely to keep up with the demands of my stove. Alf's labors would insulate me against the day I might not find time to chop wood, a day when I had visitors who didn't care to chop wood, or that day Father Larkin would come by and take me to Nuchatlitz.

After they had finished their self-appointed tasks, they changed into swim suits to enjoy the cool green waters of the cove. But one can not swim comfortably for too long in northern Pacific waters. They soon found a warm place in the sun where they could stretch out and relax, letting their swim suits dry on them. Two hours slipped so quickly away. I was sorry to see them leave.

Father Larkin did come in one day to take me to Nuchatlitz, but the real red-letter day was when Frank and Sophie paddled in with their dugout canoe. A small inboard had been installed, but more often than not it wasn't functioning. Today was one of those times. They edged up to the shore and Sophie got out to anchor their rope around a boulder. Only then did Frank raise his hulking form and ease himself from the boat.

"My heart," he said. I didn't need to be reminded. Frank had complained of his heart the first time he came to the cove, and never failed to mention it on successive visits. "We have come to see you because we need help," he continued. His slow guttural sing-song was music in itself. "Yes. I need pants." And he turned to show me.

He did need pants. The whole backside was missing. He needed shorts too. I hadn't known what to do with Wally's clothes after he died. Not wanting to offend anyone if they didn't want them, I'd packed them away. Now they were wanted and needed, and should fit, I decided, studying Frank's frame. I gave him not only pants and shorts, but shirts and shoes and socks as well.

Frank's sober brown face eased into a smile. "It's good I wear Dr. Flynn's clothes," he said. "He was my friend."

"He would want you to have them, Frank," I agreed. "I'm glad you came for them."

"We have time to stay." He continued talking almost as if I hadn't spoken. The clothes had been accepted, a statement made, the subject closed. Neither of us would ever mention it again. "Today the sea will not get rough. I tell my wife, 'We will have dinner with our friend.' "

"I'm glad. It's not fun to always eat alone."

"Yes. I tell my wife it is not good we let Mrs. Flynn be alone all the time. She is not too big to look after herself."

I checked a smile. Frank was dead serious, and never would I offend either him or Sophie, though I considered myself quite capable. Frank took no notice of my restrained smile. He was talking to Sophie in their own tongue. She nodded, got back in the canoe and, reaching under a board that served as a seat, brought out a small salmon which she held out to me.

"We catch it before we come here," Frank announced. "We think you like."

"Indeed I do like. We'll have a grand feast."

Sophie jabbered happily while we prepared and then ate our meal, the best part of which was their donation. Sophie reminded me of a wren, the quick turns of her head, the eager flash in her eyes, and especially the happy chatter. Now and again Frank translated, if he thought it was something I should know. Mostly, he just listened, a smile lighting his face, a nod in agreement, and I was aware of how very special she was to him.

CHAPTER 4

Return of the Pigeon

Could it be August already? The yellow leaves on my maple tree and the shortening days persuaded me it was. There was a bit of sadness in acknowledging the fact. I had reached the halfway point in a summer I wanted never to end.

A walk, I decided, would surely dispel the gloom. I strolled along, stopping to watch an eagle soar overhead and to assure a blue heron—who scolded me in a deep coarse croak—that I meant him no harm. He didn't believe me and his wings flapped, seemingly in slow motion, as he sought the high branches of a distant cedar tree. Black crows, selecting choice morsels from my clam bed, side-stepped to let me go by. How truly I had become a part of their worldl! The knowledge brought a smile to my lips and a lift to my spirits. After all, the summer was only half gone.

And then I heard it: the distant drone of a plane. Was it ... could it be the *Pigeon?* When Wally died I asked Father Lobsinger, who had first directed us to the cove, if the Catholic mission at Kakawis, Christie School, would like our plane. He said yes.

I listened intently. Definitely, it had to be the *Pigeon*. I couldn't mistake the drone of an engine that, over the years, had become so familiar.

Ah! There she was, soaring in over the treetops at the south end of the cove. I waved as she passed overhead and out over the inlet to make a landing. Father Lobsinger, at half tide, would have to feel his way in. I watched him maneuver around my reefs, delighted with his handling of the plane. He cut the engine then and, using his rudders, steered the *Pigeon* up onto the float Wally had designed for her.

"By the heaven," Father Lobsinger called through the open window, "You're looking great."

"And feeling great," I replied.

"Well then, run and pack your bag, quick-like. I'm taking you down to Christie for a few days. My parents and two of my aunts from Ontario are out for a visit. They'd like to meet you."

"Okay!" But then I hesitated. "Slim . . . "

"When was he here last?"

"Day before yesterday."

"No worry then. I'll have you back before he's due in again."

Christie School on Meares Island, about fifteen minutes by speedboat from the fishing village of Tofino, had become a second home. I'd gone there the first time because I'd been needed. I'd gone again last winter because I loved it. The children would all be home now, as would most of the Indian staff. And the Sisters who taught the children would have gone to their Motherhouse in Los Angeles. This was strictly a fun trip.

As we flew southeast along the rugged west coast of Vancouver Island, I recalled some of the history of Christie School. Back in the 1890's a school for the Indian children of this isolated coast became the dream of the Reverend Father A. J. Brabant. It was a time of tribal wars; a time when the white man was a hated intruder. Nevertheless, Father Brabant persisted in his dream. The place he had in mind was Kakawis, *Place of many berries.*

Reverend A. Christie, Bishop of Victoria and Vancouver Island, approved of the plan. With what little money the Victoria parish could afford, plus a small grant from the Federal Government, the land was pre-empted and arrangements made to ship the necessary lumber on the first available schooner. Two carpenters went along to build the school.

I wondered at Father Brabant's choice of Kakawis for the new school. Was it audacity, foresight, or a combination of both? I recalled the first time I'd really given any thought to the school. Father Lobsinger had hitched a ride down with Wally and me in the *Pigeon*. There was a rowboat anchored out in the bay.

"Just let me off there," he said.

"But how will you ever get to shore?" I protested, noting there were no oars in the boat.

Oars could tempt someone to borrow the boat, Father Lobsinger explained, "But don't worry," he continued, laughing at my concern, "someone will be out to pick me up."

I still felt guilty leaving him there. A more inaccessible place for a school I couldn't imagine. Fortunately, Father Brabant's assessment was more astute than mine. The school was built.

Shortly afterwards Bishop Christie was promoted to the archiepiscopacy of the state of Oregon. In Portland he succeeded in interesting the Benedictine Fathers at Mount Angel in the proposed mission school. In early May, 1900, four Sisters and two priests arrived at Kakawis. The school, a modest building, was there, but where were the pupils?

The older Indians resisted the idea of a school. The boys would be made to wear pants—an abomination. The girls would be fed bread made of flour mixed with fine glass and sand, so the stories went. The school opened with three apprehensive pupils. Gradually the objections of other parents were overcome and soon the school boasted forty pupils, staring wide-eyed at these Sisters and priests who spoke a strange language. Drawings on the blackboard affected some understanding. The children were quick-witted and eager and a friendly rapport developed.

The parents saw that their children were well cared for and happy. The enrolment at the school increased, wings were added, and a second storey, then a third. In 1938 the Benedictines were recalled to Oregon and the Missionary Oblates of Mary Immaculate took over at Christie.

The Oblates found themselves in charge of a rambling three-storey white frame building with classrooms, playrooms, dormitories, kitchen and dining areas and, in the south wing on the second floor, a lovely chapel where children had learned to love the "white man's God", where they had worshiped and been baptized. During my first winter at Christie I took Instruction and was baptized into the Church with Rose's oldest daughter, Vera, serving as my sponsor. For me, as with all who have had contacts with Christie, there are many happy memories.

Father Lobsinger nudged me. "By the heaven, you're quiet. I hope you aren't having second thoughts. We're almost there, you know."

"I'm torn between wanting to get there and wishing this flight could go on and on."

"My feelings exactly. There's something special about sitting up here in this old bird. Ah well, here we are."

Indeed we were. Christie School, dominating a two

hundred foot bluff, with forested Lone Cone Mountain as a backdrop, had a majestic, almost a Tudor appearance. On a small knoll below the bluff, a Crucifix stood guard over the bay. It was a lovely bay, shielded from the full force of the Pacific by several islands. The waters seemed quiet now, deceptively so, for when the tide was high and the winds whistled through the trees, the sea pounded the beach with a steady, unrelenting roar.

Father circled and gunned the engine and as we swooped down for a landing, I saw a figure hurry to the beach. Probably Brother O'Brien. To me, he was Mr. Kakawis. Priests and other Brothers came, stayed on a few years and left, but not Brother O'Brien. I doubted Christie could function without him. His know-how was nothing short of remarkable. If there was a break in the water line he repaired it. If the lights in the school went out, there was an urgent call for Brother O'Brien. The balky old kitchen range, a huge affair with side-by-side ovens, had been converted from wood to oil. No one but Brother could restrain its vexing eccentricities. In the laundry room were two commercial-size cylinder machines surely dating back to the early 1900's. To keep upwards of two hundred people in clothing, bedding and towels those machines must be kept turning.

But no, that running figure wasn't Brother O'Brien. From the Oblates rec room came a blast of music. Brother O'Brien, using an old record player and an amplifier, delighted in serenading guests. He didn't often obtain the latest hits but the music had rhythm and, more importantly, it was loud. It filled the bay, bombarding us with sound.

I grinned at Father Lobsinger. "Brother sure knows how to make you feel welcome."

"Yes, up to his usual tricks."

"Nice tricks. I like them. Is that Father Noonan on the tractor?"

"It is. I don't know how we'd manage without that tractor. No job seems too big for it to handle."

Brother O'Brien and the priests had built a platform for the *Pigeon* as there was no place in the bay where it could be safely anchored. Had there been, it still would not have been a satisfactory mooring, for salt water is notably hard on aluminum floats.

I watched Father Noonan attach a tow chain to the platform and drag it into the sea. Water surged around the wheels of the tractor.

"If the sea gets in the engine, it'll wreck it," I fretted.

"Don't worry. He knows how far he can go."

He did know. He turned in his seat and waved. Father Lobsinger taxied in and up onto the platform. Father Noonan put the tractor into gear and pulled us from the sea and across the wide expanse of sand almost to the foot of the bluff. It was quite a feat. The yellow *Pigeon*, I figured, must weigh all of 4000 pounds.

"All the work you have to go to, getting the *Pigeon* in and out of the water, I'm surprised you still want her," I told Father Noonan.

His grin was reassuring, but then he said, "Your added weight did make the job a bit tougher." He grinned again. "Good to see you."

"Good to be here, too."

"Hop on the tractor. I'll give you a ride up the hill."

"Thanks, but I'll take the path up the bluff."

The path was steep, and rocks and roots got in the way. I was out of breath when I reached the top. Some hundred or so yards from the school the bluff dipped to the beach where a mountain stream bubbled into the salt-chuck. On the other side of the stream was another rise which extended to a point about a mile out into the bay.

Sometime, Brother O'Brien had assured me, a pier would be built at that point. For the present they had to be satisfied with a road of sorts that led from the stream and up a steep incline, passing on the way the barn-like gym, where basketball and volleyball games were played. The tractor, with both Fathers on board, reached the school ahead of me.

Father Lobsinger had my bag. "I'll take you in the kitchen door," he said. "Mary can show you which room you'll have."

The kitchen at Christie is Mary Hay's domain. Her home in the Indian village of Opitsat, on the south side of Meares Island, is about a forty-five minute walk from the school. I love Mary. She is the hardest-working woman I've ever known. As I entered the kitchen she came to meet me, her face one big smile. We embraced, then giggled, momentarily at a loss for words.

"I'll take your bag," she said then.

Side by side we walked down the corridor that separated the kitchen from the priests', the Sisters', and the staff's dining rooms. We passed through the girls' dining room, then up the stairs to the second floor. Ceilings were extravagantly high. My room was on the second floor looking out over the bay.

"Come down to the kitchen when you're unpacked," she said. "Everybody is around someplace."

I didn't hurry after Mary left me. I stood gazing out the window, reflecting on the beauty of this lovely place. Then my thoughts turned to Mary. "I'd better be getting down to the kitchen," I reminded myself, glancing at my watch. "Maybe Mary can use some help."

Mary had plenty of help, I discovered. Father Lobsinger's mother, Leone, and both his aunts, Agnes and Beatrice, had had the same thought I'd had, only sooner. Mary could probably have done as well without any of us, but Mary is a social person. She enjoyed our chatter, not minding the confusion.

"This is the most fascinating place," Mrs. Lobsinger told me after we had introduced ourselves. "When those lovely odours from Mary's cooking start floating up the stairs I just can't stay away." Agnes and Beatrice agreed.

Certainly no place is more conducive to getting to know one another than a big old kitchen permeated with tantalizing smells. A big pot of coffee on the back of the stove was added inducement. We sipped at mugs, getting in each other's way and laughing over the encounter. Our tongues worked faster than our hands.

In the midst of all the confusion Brother O'Brien appeared. "Looks like a party," he said. "I'll join you. Mary, how about a couple of your famous cookies?"

"Brother," she protested, "it's almost supper time."

"Is it now? But you wouldn't be denying a starving man a single crumb, would you?"

Straightaway he went to the five-gallon lard pail that Mary kept filled with cookies and helped himself. It was a game they played. I knew from past experience. Brother O'Brien always came in early for coffee and cookies, but they in no way altered his appetite for supper.

Irish and Indian, but they were really much alike, I decided. They both worked hard, but a cheerful attitude was common to both.

That night before I went to bed I knelt in front of my open window to look out at a star-sparkled sky. The roar of the sea, mysteriously muffled by the night, was music to my ears. When I climbed into bed I could hear it still, a lullaby that gently nudged me into dreamland. Some time later I awakened. My room was filled with the most delectable odour. I knew what it was. Martin always baked bread at night after everyone had gone to bed.

Resisting those odours was impossible. I got up and

dressed and ran down to the bakery. Martin was pulling trays of golden-crusted loaves of bread from giant built-in ovens. The smell was almost overwhelming.

He caught sight of me standing in the doorway and smiled a welcome.

"I though you would be down," he said. "I baked rolls specially. Coffee's hot."

"Mmm! Smells so good! How could I stay away?"

Martin Saxby was originally from Kyuquot, north of my cove. But now, like Mary, he had made Christie his home. He was soft-spoken and unassuming, merely grinning when anyone told him he was the best baker in the country. The ultimate compliment was to leave your warm bed and join him for a midnight snack. Martin and I had barely seated ourselves at a small corner table when Brother O'Brien bounded into the room.

We sat there for the better part of an hour, laughing and talking, eating hot rolls dripping with butter, consuming innumerable cups of coffee. Yet, when I crawled back into bed I was soon asleep, soothed again by the sounds of the sea.

Those days at Christie went by so fast. New seatcovers for the *Pigeon* was a major project and everyone joined in the effort, except me. Sewing was not one of my accomplishments. In the late afternoons or evenings we went fishing, or at least for a boat ride. Mr. Lobsinger was delighted when he caught a salmon and even more delighted when Mary served it for supper the following evening. I was almost sorry when it was time for me to go home.

I was quiet on the trip home, reflecting on all the fun and confusion I was leaving behind. I even felt a bit sad. But when we circled the cove, those feelings vanished. What a beautiful spot—and it was *mine*.

CHAPTER 5

The Gift

Strange, I thought. When I was at Christie I had enjoyed being a part of all that went on there. Back here at the cove, memories were fading, as the memories of my life in Seattle had faded. Not that I ceased loving any one of my family or friends. It was more an acceptance of this small world, a sense of delightful complacency, that blocked out those other worlds. Slim came in on schedule and Father Larkin whisked in and out. Other than that I was alone and yet not alone, for this world I lived in was an entity in itself with life so abundant it staggered the imagination.

Bees hovered over blackberry blossoms, their hummm a busy, pleasant sound. My filberts were ripening, provoking an on-going quarrel between the jays and the squirrels. Many times I watched a jay jab his beak into a still soft hull in search of the tender kernel inside while the squirrels chattered in noisy indignation. Tessie and Jasper, my audacious mink, must have invited all their relatives to share the cove. Someone had once asked me about trapping mink here at the cove. "No way!" I'd replied. "I like my fur coats running free."

The berries on my mountain ash had turned a bright red, a feast set for the crows which came in unheralded numbers, their hoarse caw, caw continuing from morning till night. Seagulls circled the cove in search of juicy morsels from the sea. And there was Minniebelle. She did not scream or caw or chatter, but her rustle in the bushes, her deliberate pacing on the kitchen roof, her persistent watch in the plum tree, kept me aware of her presence.

I drifted along with the days, so immersed in my world that when Father Larkin came in one day I was startled. He arrived with such speed and flourish I swear my reefs had to duck. The Indians, I reflected, were more cautious.

"Get yourself ready," he greeted me. "We're going to Nuchatlitz."

No wasted words, but beneath that gruff exterior was a gentleness and a sensitivity that came to the surface in so many unexpected ways. He was so much like Wally: kind, considerate, with the same roguish Irish grin, the twinkle in the eyes, the wavy black hair, even a similar stocky build. I wished Wally could have known him better. Father had been assigned to our area just before Wally died. Too bad. They could have been such good friends.

******

There were many to greet us at the dock in Nuchatlitz. I was especially delighted to see Vera. She took her responsibility as my sponsor seriously. Had she suggested to Father Larkin that I should come to Mass? After all, as a fairly recent convert, I must not be allowed to backslide.

Vera had graduated from the eighth grade at Christie and had gone on to high school, attending the Indian mission school at Kamloops in interior British Columbia. What a lovely girl, I thought, so unaware of a charm and a beauty that set her apart. She resembled Rose, but was more slight, quick, eager, her flashing smile an indication of an inherent joy, an enthusiasm for living and learning. If Vera felt a responsibility towards me, I felt a like responsibility in not ever letting her down.

Rose's kitchen was crowded with all her children home and with their friends running in and out. There was laughter and the constant hum of voices—soft guttural tones, none of the shrillness I objected to in the voices of so many Caucasian youngsters. Rose maintained order in a voice that was low, but firm. I saw an Indian basket of a type one could use for shopping, sturdily woven of cedar bark and sea grasses. I went over and picked it up.

"Vera!" I exclaimed, "I've never seen a basket like this, with the name of your village worked right into the design."

"Do you like it?" she asked.

"I do," And then the church bell rang. I set the basket down and headed for the church with Rose and Vera.

Father Larkin didn't seem in much of a hurry this day. We lingered after Mass, and then there were more families to visit. I made my usual rounds, staying longest with Josephine Paul—Jo, I called her. Jo carried herself with a certain dignity, almost a sophistication due, probably, to her many years at Christie. Her hair was pulled up into a French roll, soft waves deflecting any hint of severity. She was slight, finely boned—a most attractive women. She and Rose were cousins. Joe, her father, was Moses' brother.

I forgot about time until Father Larkin walked in the door. "Women!" he said. "Giggle, giggle, giggle. For the life of me I don't know what you find to talk about." But the wide Irish grin told us that whatever it was, it was okay with him. "We'd best be getting back, I think."

Jo walked with us down to the dock. Rose and Vera

joined us, and more youngsters than I could keep track of.

A few days later a speedboat skirted my reefs and entered the cove. It was Pat's boat, but that wasn't Pat in the boat. As it came in closer I recognized Rose and Vera and two of the younger children.

"Today Pat isn't working at the logging camp," Rose greeted me. "We borrow his boat." And she laughed, happy laughter. Rose would have visited me often if only she'd had a boat. Many times she had told me so.

"All the men go fishing in their trollers. The women have to stay home."

But today she had a boat. Taken in by her joy, I forgot Vera and the youngsters. But then Vera came to stand beside us, flashing that smile no one could ignore or resist. The children had run off around the cove in search of blackberries. I gave Vera a hug, which she failed to return, her hands remaining behind her back. I was puzzled. Vera caught my look and laughed outright.

"I bring you a present," she said, and she held out the basket I had so admired, the one with the word *Nuchatlitz* woven into the design.

"Oh!" I gasped. "I never expected . . . It's so special. How can you give it up?"

We want you to have it," Vera said shyly, and Rose nodded agreement. My joy was their joy. The basket was special, but my neighbours at Nuchatlitz were special too.

******

September sneaked in through the fog that had hung around during August, generally clinging to the far shore of Esperanza Inlet, always dissipating before noon. Now it closed in on me, shutting out the world. When the fog

left, the rains came down and I tracked in evergreen
needles and fallen leaves from my maple and filbert trees.
It was a messy time and a noisy time. The wind whipped
the sea and it pounded my rocky shore. My streams raced
down precipitous inclines fanning out on the beach to
join the sea. It was an exhilarating time, also a demanding time: carrying in wood, carrying out ashes, sweeping
up the mess, bailing the boat.... Slosh, slosh, slosh,
more often wet than dry, but withal that glorious feeling
that comes with physical work.

One day, quite suddenly, the rain gave way to the sun,
but it was not a warm sun. There was a coolness in the
air, a feeling that fall would not delay too long. Vera
would have returned to Kamloops, the others to Christie,
reminding me that I, too, soon must leave. I pushed the
thought aside, not ready yet to surrender to the calendar.
I padded down the forested path to the outside beach
where I could see far up Esperanza Inlet in either direction, and saw a boat. Pat's? Yes, it was Pat's. I turned and
ran, back along the forest path, back around the curve of
the cove, right to my steps where I knew Pat would pull
in and anchor. I barely beat him. His Vera was with him.

Mrs. Flynn," he said with a grin, "you are going to run
yourself down."

I grinned in return, shook my head and invited them
up for coffee.

They accepted my invitation, but as we sat drinking
coffee I sensed a change. As the years had passed Pat and
Vera had found it easier to talk with me. Today Pat had
little to say. There were no shy giggles from Vera. It was
strange, I thought, how my Indian friends could be so
out-going, and at the same time shy. Today it was as if
they were waiting. But waiting for what?

At length Pat set his cup down and stood. "I think we
will go now."

Had I missed my cue? This visit had not gone as it should. They seemed almost troubled. I pondered their unusual behavior as I led the way down to the beach. Pat started to release his anchor rope, then hesitated and turned to me.

"We come to talk," he said.

"Pat, I wish you would. Let's sit here on the beach. It's much nicer down here."

Pat nodded and we arranged ourselves on the rocks. Pat and Vera seemed more at ease here than in my kitchen. Still Pat did not speak. I didn't prod. When he was ready he would talk.

"We have a worry," he said finally.

"Can I help?"

No, Mrs. Flynn, but we would like to know if you think we decide right. Indian people go to pubs and get very drunk."

I nodded. "I know."

"There is a law," he continued. "Indians cannot take any liquor away from the pub. When the pub closes they go sleep all night on their boat. They get sober, then go home."

Pat sat silent a few minutes. Vera said nothing. I waited.

"Now there will be a new law." Pat seemed almost to be talking to himself. "Indians can take liquor home like the white man. He can be drunk all the time. In Nuchatlitz some of us want to keep the old law."

I nodded again, remembering a sign near the dock: *No intoxicating liquors permitted in Nuchatlitz village.* Probably the priests had been the instigators, but the villagers had taken pride in that sign. The first time Wally and I had visited Nuchatlitz, old Chief Michael had taken pains to point it out to us. In part, it was maybe a warning to the white man: *Don't bring any of your liquor here.*

Pat tossed a stone into the water, watched it sink to the bottom. I saw he was deeply troubled.

"Some in Nuchatlitz like the new law. They like to be drunk. Then it will not be good in Nuchatlitz. Vera and I talk a long time. Nuchatlitz is our home. We don't like to go away."

"But you think you must leave. Is that right, Pat?"

"Yes, Mrs. Flynn. Vera and I don't want to drink."

"Where will you go?"

"We talk to Rose and to Jo. Jo will ask Father Noonan. We can work at Christie."

"I'm sure you've made the right decision, Pat. And I'll be glad if you go to Christie. You and Vera are my good friends. I'd be sorry not to see you any more. At Christie I can see you."

They smiled, both of them. They had wanted to talk with someone . . . not Indian. Their decision was good. They were sure now. Pat released his anchor rope.

"See you," he said. Vera waved and they were on their way.

But I sat on the beach a long while, fighting a feeling of futility. What could I do? Drinking had long been a problem, a problem that would be aggravated by the availability of more liquor. . . .

CHAPTER 6

Nit Picking

Seattle's main attraction for me was Maureen and the children. In 1960 Maureen had come to the cove with a year-old son, Greg. Now there were Pam and Jeff also, towheads all, in striking contrast to the brown-skinned, black-haired children of Nuchatlitz, but just as lovable. I adored them. Greg, now five, lorded it over three year old Pam, and Jeff, who was barely two.

The first few weeks slipped by, almost without my realizing it, as I played with the children and chatted with Maureen. But then the rains came and my spirit rebelled. Raindrops bouncing up from cement didn't hold the same charm as raindrops filtering through evergreen needles or spattering the waters of the cove with millions of miniature whirlpools. The call of the coast became ever more urgent.

"You may as well go, Mom," Maureen told me. There was laughter in her voice. She understood. "Just come back for Christmas. Okay?"

Christie School at Kakawis was my destination.

******

There was never TOO much help at Christie. I never

51

gave a thought to what my job would be ... more than likely, a conglomeration. My first thought was to get settled in my room. I generally had the same one, a long narrow room with an exorbitantly high ceiling and a steam radiator in front of one of the double windows that overlooked the bay. It contained a portable closet, a turn-of-the-century dresser and two twin-size beds. Sharing the room was sometimes a necessity.

I set my bag down by the dresser. I admired that dresser. There was none other like it in the school. There were two drawers just above floor level. Above the drawers on the left was a tall, narrow mirror. On the right side a door opened into a small cupboard. It pleased me I had the use of this dresser when I was here. Once I'd had a room with no mirror, with calamitous results. I had attended Mass with the hem of my dress caught in my belt. Maybe that was why I'd been given this room. I was not about to quarrel with the reason however.

I didn't have to wait too long to learn what my first job would be. Sister Ruth Ann was soon knocking at my door. She taught the first and second grades and was also responsible for her girls outside the classroom. Brothers watched over the boys. Each Sister taught two grades and shared the dormitory with the girls, their privacy assured to a degree by partitions whose walls did not extend to the ceiling. A door could be shut, but the lowered partitions were a safety valve. Any child who cried out during the night was certain to be heard.

"We have a real problem this fall," Sister Ruth Ann told me after we'd greeted each other. "I've never known such an infestation of nits. We've paired the older children off. They inspect each other daily and we check them all once a week, but my little ones have to be inspected daily ... by me. I tell you, I see nits in my sleep." She laughed then, a hearty, contagious laugh and I knew the situation hadn't demoralized her. "You're not shocked?" she asked.

I shook my head. "I sympathize. I'll never forget one day at the cove. I awoke in the morning with the strangest feeling. My scalp seemed to be moving. I put my hand up to my head, thinking to hold it still. Something was moving all right, but it wasn't my scalp."

Sister Ruth Ann's eyes were twinkling. A hand in front of her mouth suppressed her laughter.

"You dare laugh!" I threatened her. "I'd been to the village," I continued. "As you know, the children are socuddly. I held them on my lap. Sure, I kissed them. Our hair touched and the lice hopped across. Oh, you can laugh?"

She did, and I continued my recital. "I ran down to the kitchen, as close to hysteria as I've ever been. No idea what to do. Then I had a thought. In Wally's bag there was a can of the spray we'd used to kill lice and fleas on animals. I didn't give a darn what effect such a spray might have on a human. I doused my head good, then doused it again. There was a tingling sensation ... but my scalp no longer walked. I don't need to tell you I still had a problem. The eggs, or young lice ... nits, you call them, had probably rubbed off on my bedding. I carried it all down to the beach and spread it out on the rocks. I sprayed and sprayed. Left it on several hours, then scrubbed everything, including my own head. Well, the spray didn't seem to do me any harm so the next time I was in Seattle I ordered more."

Sister Ruth Ann laughed again. "Anything can be overcome, I guess," she said. "Do you have a can of that spray with you?"

"I'm never without it."

"Then I'm safe in asking for your help with the children. The little ones need help with their baths and shampoos. They get a lice shampoo once a week, regular shampoos daily."

The east end of the girls' dining room had been partitioned off to accommodate a tub area, each tub enclosed in semi-walls to insure privacy. I never counted all the tubs but three were reserved for Sister Ruth Ann's charges; probably twenty to twenty five little girls. The nit session, as I called it, was a particularly happy time of the day. Tub bathing was a luxury unknown in the coastal villages that were home to these children. The large porcelain tubs with their claw feet might look grotesque alongside their more modern counterparts, but to these children they were a delight.

Two children could fit comfortably in each tub with room to spare to kick and splash. Supple brown bodies squirmed and rolled in ecstacy, accompanied by soft gurgles of laughter. Since the walls of the cubicles didn't reach the ceiling I could hear what was happening in all three. They soaped each other, but the shampooing I reserved for myself, scrubbing each head thoroughly as they sat in the tub, rinsing until the water ran clear.

"A-ach, Mrs. Flynn! You get soap in my eyes," Rita protested.

"Bend your head down. Wring out your washcloth and hold it tight over your eyes."

"I forget, Mrs. Flynn."

It was part of the game. They'd been told, but to be told again was more fun.

"Okay, now. Hop out and towel yourself dry."

"N-a-ah, Mrs. Flynn. I don't want."

"Come now, Patty, you too, Rita. Doreen and Caroline are waiting for their turn."

I can think of no better way to establish a meaningful relationship than by giving baths. There is also no surer way of acquiring a backache. When finally I'd climb the stairs to my room I'd stretch and wiggle my shoulders, in an effort to remove the kinks.

Nits aren't so easily eradicated, but eventually we were able to dispense with daily shampoos. Daily encounters, however, were not dispensed with. When school was out for the day they'd gather around me. We'd run to the beach. A little rain never stopped us. We were all dressed warmly in jackets and boots. As we hiked along over the sand some of the children clung to my arms. Others ran ahead, or trailed behind, searching for treasures, shells and bits of drift, which they presented with shy adoration, their faces lighting up when they saw I was pleased. Other times we walked the short road to the beach. They'd run ahead and hide in the bush, popping out unexpectedly, laughing gleefully when I was properly startled.

One day after a run on the beach we all stormed into the kitchen for a snack. "What are you kids hanging onto Mrs. Flynn for?" Sister Emelia teased. "She's malmethne."

Malmethne! When the white man came to the west coast of Vancouver Island in 1778 their ships were anchored off Yuquot in Nootka Sound. White men on a floating house... malmethne. But during the years the Indians came to distrust the white man. Malmethne had become a derogatory term, reserved for those white people the Indians felt were unworthy of their friendship.

The children were shaking their heads now, their dark eyes serious. "No, S'ter. She not malmethne."

"Of course she's malmethne," Sister Emelia teased.

"No! She not!"

"What is she then?" Sister demanded.

"She Indian!" It was a chorus. Heads nodded agreement and they giggled their merriment.

My curly blond hair and fair skin had made no difference. I was one of them.

I didn't spend all my time with the children. I still helped in the kitchen, as I had the first time I'd come to Christie. I worked with the older girls preparing vegetables, or mixing cakes and cookies. Often I leaned over the long work table with Mary and Jo and Sister Emelia as we worked out on paper the menu for the day, or for days ahead. Mid-morning and mid-afternoon we'd stop for a coffee break, generally joined by Brother O'Brien and other members of the staff. Sister Emelia would desert us after the break. She divided her time between the kitchen and the sewing room, a place I avoided. The older girls took naturally to sewing. I admired their work, but with no wish to compete.

Sometimes I wandered over to the laundry, a huge room smelling of soap and Purex. A dampness seemed to hang in the air. The men were in charge here. The work was heavy and the machinery cantankerous. The dryer never failed to startle and astonish me. Shaped like a flying saucer atop a pedestal, it whirled with a speed the eye could scarcely follow.

"Good grief, Brother O'Brien," I bellowed above the racket, "some day that thing is going to take right off into space."

It never did. It did remove the soppiness from its contents. I helped the girls carry baskets of damp laundry either to the drying room where it was strung out on racks or, if the day was sunny and warm, up the outside stairs to the flat roof over the north end of the building. We'd walk to the roof's edge to reel in the long wire lines. In the spring wild daffodils grew in profusion under these lines. Color during the winter was provided by an assortment of clothing, bedding, towels and linens flapping in the wind.

Esther was in charge of the drying room. An oil stove set against one wall helped with the drying and took some of the dampness out of the air. There were also a number of ironing boards which were constantly in use. After the laundry had been dried and ironed it had to be sorted and carried to specific storerooms where the Sisters and Brothers kept what was needed for their charges. I enjoyed working with Esther. She and Joe, who worked in the laundry, were probably the only ones at Christie older than I. She was a gentle person, but with a firmness that tolerated no slip-shod work. It was good, I thought, that here at Christie discipline of the students was so often meted out by the elders from their own villages. Every west coast village had a representative on the staff—so that almost every youngster had a parent, an aunt, an uncle, or some adult they knew well. For the little ones there were also older brothers and sisters who had helped care for them at home. As a result there were few cases of homesickness.

One of the younger boys delighted me with his frank confession. I saw him peeking around the kitchen door. The kitchen was off-bounds except during snack time.

"Did you want something?" I asked him.

"Yes. Father say I have to say I am sorry."

"Oh! What did you do?"

"I committed adultery. I stole an apple out of the kitchen."

Adultery! Of course. In the kitchen we all were adults. "And are you sorry?" I asked him.

"Yes. Father say, 'Next time you want an apple, ask. They might give you one.' "

"I see. Well, you run along now and come back at snack time. Maybe then there will be apples for all of you."

CHAPTER 7

Christie Celebrations

I was glad I'd arrived at Kakawis before Halloween. At Christie School Halloween is the most exciting day of the year; not wondrous like Christmas, not solemn like graduation; just fun. There were jack-o-lanterns and treats. There were tricks and firecrackers. The priests and Brothers donned masks and popped out at the children from the most unexpected places. The children quivered gleefully, and more than one was heard to remark, "A-ach, Father, I know you." Father Noonan, I was sure, was enjoying this as much as his victims.

Then there was spook alley. On the south side of the gym was a long narrow hallway. What its original purpose was would be hard to conjecture, but on Halloween eve the spirits held forth. Brother O'Brien masterminded this den of witchery. With the walls draped and the lights off, the alleyway was inky-black. At impromptu moments a light would flash on and the head of a ghost or witch would appear accompanied by horrendous laughter. A hand would reach out to clutch the victim's. There was a buzzing sound and a tingling sensation. I know, because I, too, visited spook alley. It extended the full length of the basketball court, allowing for plenty of surprises. The kids felt their way down and back, and emerged with eyes as big as saucers.

"I got scared. I want to go again."

When one is young and imaginative there is a shivery delight in being scared. . . . Not frightened—just scared. There is a difference. If you are frightened it can go on and on, but if you are simply scared, it is only for the moment. Halloween is a time to be scared.

Halloween, however, didn't have a corner on the fun times. Sports nights were special. The pounding of running feet, the thump, thump of the basketball, the animated cheers of onlookers encouraging the players, set up a vibration that reached to the rafters of the old gym.

Everyone took part in these events but care was taken that the teams were evenly matched. Sister Peter Damian, who taught the seventh and eighth grades, excelled in both basketball and volleyball. Her long black habit was no deterrent. She out-ran and out-jumped the best. Watching her laughing and shouting and cheering her teammates on, it was hard to reconcile her with a more serious side: that of Sister Superior.

When the weather and the tides cooperated Sister Laura and her fifth and sixth grade students organized picnics and baseball games on the hard sandy beach. Sports held a high priority for the Indian children. They loved the action and the competition. Sports drew teachers and students together; a common bond.

Sister Mary Jordan wasn't athletic, but she could sing and strum a mean guitar. Her third and fourth grade students led in the singing while still taking part in the games.

Sister Columbiere was always on hand, often taking part in the game. Besides instructing sewing classes, she was also school nurse. Those who needed attention for cuts, headaches, whatever, would line up outside the door to await their turn. Temperatures were taken and if a child was really sick, a trip to the hospital at Tofino was prescribed. It wasn't long before I was convinced her gentle smile and her caring were as effective as the medications she dispensed.

One Friday evening, since there would be no school the next day, Father Noonan ran an old movie. This was a big night, complete with treats. The film, a cowboy and Indian Western, aroused a lot of interest. The younger children didn't understand the show, but they stayed until the end, ensconced on someone's lap, their head cradled against a shoulder, or crouched at someone's feet, their heads resting against knees. The older students wildly cheered on the Indians, to such an extent it was impossible to hear the dialogue. It didn't really matter. The action was the thing.

Again, on a Friday evening, we had a dancing party for the seventh and eighth grades. Brother O'Brien brought the phonograph down to the recreation room in the north wing. When the music started, the boys rose on cue, each one asking a girl to dance. In spite of poker-straight bodies and serious expressions, they made a lovely picture, the boys in suits and ties, the girls in colorful dresses. As their confidence increased, their bodies relaxed to the music. Grins replaced the serious expressions. The measured steps were incompatible with the impetuosity of their native dances, but the laughter that rippled through the room was ample proof they were having fun.

After the dance everyone hurried to the kitchen to sample the treats Mary and Jo had prepared: hot chocolate, sandwiches, cookies. Only Brother O'Brien, Sister Emelia and I remained behind. Brother O'Brien was sorting out his records.

"Don't put them away, Brother," Sister Emelia begged. "Play one for us."

He nodded and grinned and the lilting sounds of The Tennessee Waltz swelled in the now empty room.

Sister Emelia grabbed me around the waist. "Come on. Let's dance."

"Sister Emelia," I protested, "I haven't danced in years."

"Neither have I. So now is the time."

Sister Emelia was the youngest of the Sisters, not much over twenty, I judged. Of Mexican descent, she was quick and eager in whatever she undertook. Her dark brown-neyes now sparkled with mischief. It was impossible to resist her. How she could dance! She spun me around the room as if I was no more than a feather.

"Play another, Brother," she ordered when the waltz ground to a stop. "You're good," she said to me.

I was soon circling the room with an abandonment that equalled hers. For over an hour Brother O'Brien obliged with one record after another. Finally he rebelled.

"If you girls want to dance all night, you'll have to play the records yourself. I'm hungry. By now," he observed, "the kids will have eaten everything in sight."

"Don't worry, Brother," Sister Emelia reassured him. "I'll fix us something."

The dominant theme through most of November and December was the preparation for the annual Christmas program which would be presented the week before Christmas. Each Sister was responsible for the play or skit her students would perform. Natural-born actors, and with no inhibitions, they responded with unabashed enthusiasm. Sister Columbiere fashioned the costumes.

The anticipated day finally arrived. Visitors began gathering in the early afternoon. They came from nearby Indian villages. They came also from Tofino: fishermen, merchants and their families, and as many of the hospital staff as could be dispensed with. Christie had a reputation for putting on outstanding programs.

All day long there was noise and confusion and unabated excitement. Chairs had to be set up in the rec room. The Brothers and the older boys had built a stage. As we gathered in the rec room that evening there was a babble of voices, subdued laughter, and the scraping of many chairs. Then Father Noonan climbed up onto the stage and there was an immediate hush. He welcomed the visitors and told them how hard the young people had worked. Then he stepped down and two senior boys drew back the curtains.

The young actors responded on cue. Confident, oblivious to all but the part they were playing they told the old story of Joseph and Mary and the baby Jesus. There were variations as the different age groups presented their interpretations. Sister Ruth Ann's first and second graders were totally at ease. They spoke as they would normally.

"Hurry up, Mary. You not suppose to have your baby here. We got to get to the manger."

"Hello, Wise Man. You got a present?"

As the skits came to a close, the caroling began. The children sang from their hearts, the notes sweet and mellow. And at the close of the program Santa arrived with a gift for each one.

The visitors from Tofino left then, but most of the Indian visitors stayed the night, many of them sleeping in their trollers, some finding room in the school. The next morning there was a general exodus. But many children would not go home, like my young friends from Nuchatlitz. Their parents had not come. The long voyage in stormy winter seas was a strong deterrent. These children, however, were far from sad.

"Is more better here," one of them told me. "We get

presents and good things to eat. No school now. Lots of fun."

There would be parties and singing. There would be games. There would be excursions along the beach to look for glass balls and special shells, and a day to look for just the perfect Christmas tree. On Christmas Eve there would be a party with stories and carols. On Christmas morning they would dress for Mass in their very best, to thank the baby Jesus for all their happy times.

Thinking ahead to their joy I was a bit sad at having to miss it until I reminded myself that in Maureen's home in Seattle there would be joy, too, and three very special youngsters to share it with me. Telling Christie youngsters good-by, however, wasn't easy.

Their voices, their eyes, expressed such sadness, but I knew that in five minutes after my departure they would have found a reason for joy and would be smiling again. I hugged them and kissed them and told them I'd be back.

CHAPTER 8

Arrival of the Grandchildren

That November, in Seattle, I had more evidence it was my destiny to continue spending my summers at the cove. The evidence came in a letter from Rose.

"We have a little girl, born November 24. She is a beautiful good baby. We want to name her for our friend. Her name is Lena Bethine. We hope you like that."

I did like that. I waited impatiently for summer so I could see for myself that tiny Lena Bethine.

******

Rose was so proud to show her to me. She accepted my gift, a baby-pink dress and booties to match, then put them aside with a quiet thank-you. I had eyes only for the baby. Chocolate brown eyes studied me curiously. A button of a mouth gurgled a happy goo and one little brown arm waved indecisively, as if searching for something tiny fingers could grasp. She looked so soft and cuddly, but I resisted an impulse to pick her up. An okay must come from Rose.

But Rose simply smiled that gentle smile I had come to know so well. I watched as she poured water from a teakettle into a large basin, adding cool water from a bucket, testing the water in the basin with her elbow until the degree of warmth satisfied her.

So baby was to have a bath. She loved it, gurgling and crowing, slapping the water with tiny hands, kicking her feet, until there was almost more water on the floor than in the basin. Rose toweled her dry, diapered her and put on a little undershirt, and then, surprise, the pink dress and booties. She cuddled her a moment, then held her out to me. I understood. A gift sweet and clean! Lena Bethine was my baby, not to take away of course, but for sharing with the family.

Alban had watched the entire process. "It is good," he said, and there was pure joy in his voice. "We have two Bethines in our family." And there was pure joy in my heart too.

We put a sweater on Baby Bethine and took her to Mass. She sat on my lap the whole time, perfectly content, seeming to know in her baby heart that in some way she belonged to me too.

In early June I received a letter that radically changed my rather self-indulgent life style. The letter was from Maureen.

"We want to come up for the whole summer, Mom," she wrote. "Dick's being sent to Wyoming for six weeks and is taking Greg along. I sure don't feel like sitting here chewing my nails till they get back. I'll come up now with Pam and Jeff. When Dick gets back he'll drive Greg to Vancouver and put him on a plane so he can join us. I want the kids to know there's more to living than just what we experience in Seattle."

They arrived around the middle of June, fortunately on a day when the sun had decided to poke through the clouds. The plane nudged up to the south section of my beach, which boasted gravel rather than rocks. I waded out. The pilot lifted the kids down onto the float and I carried them to shore. I waded back for their bags, then reached for Maureen's. Her way had been blocked by kids and bags.

"Don't take that one, Mom. It's too heavy," she said.

"Huh! Just because you have me bested by about seven inches! You think I'm some kind of a weakling?" I lifted up on the bag but it didn't budge.

Maureen grinned impishly, pushing at an unruly strand of blonde hair. "I think you're showing off," she said.

"What have you got in that bag?" I demanded. "Lead?"

"Books! I've decided to take evening classes at the University of Washington this fall. Figured I'd better bone up. It's been a while."

As she talked she slipped off her shoes and her hose, picked up her bag, with ease, and with a studied nonchalance, I thought, followed me to shore.

"All okay?" the pilot asked.

"Yep! And I'll be looking for you Friday."

"Right. You want to give me a shove out? And maybe you can catch the tail and swing me around."

"Well," I said, as the plane rounded the curve of the island, "now that that's taken care of, hello." And I hugged the kids and kissed them soundly.

"Grandma," Jeff said, "I sure do like to ride in that plane. Can I come again?"

"I hope so, but since you're here now maybe we should go up to the house and get something to eat. I'll bet you're hungry."

I needn't have worried about the kids' reaction to wilderness living. A wood stove and kerosene lamps were far more intriguing than an electric stove and electric lights. The old house with its log walls was much nicer than home with its flat painted walls. There were infinite reasons for running up and down stairs. Their house had no upstairs.

But it was the out-of-doors that was most enticing. They spotted Minniebelle and chased her down the path. She foiled them, flying to her favorite perch in the plum tree where she regarded them disapprovingly.

"Better get used to them, Minniebelle," I cautioned her. "They're going to be around for a while.'

They pegged stones into the water and, in turning over the stones, discovered tiny crabs scurrying about. They picked them up, let them crawl up their bare arms and shivered with delight. They searched for shells, swung from low-hanging branches, and padded noiselessly along mossy trails.

"It smells pretty up here, Grandma," Jeff told me. "I like it."

I took them out in my rowboat and both wanted to row. In the quiet waters of the cove, I taught them.

"It's hard work, Grandma," Pam observed as she plied the oars awkwardly, unable to get them to function in unison.

"Yes, it is," I agreed. "It took me a long time to learn. But you keep at it. Pretty soon you'll be surprised how easy it is."

For Jeff, rowing seemed to come naturally. He was too little, and his arms too short for those long oars, but he grasped them resolutely and, arms bent at the elbow, like a wing on either side of his head, he pulled at the oars.

"Grandma! I can do it," he yelled.

And then one day Father Larkin came in. He picked the kids up and swung them around and they thought he was the greatest. He stayed for a picnic on the beach, delighting the kids with his prowess at making a beach fire, getting them scurrying for drift. They ran, tugging at pieces too big to carry.

It had seemed a perfect day until the few minutes Father managed alone with me before he left.

"I think I should tell you this will be my last summer here," he said.

"Father! You can't mean it!"

"I'm afraid I do. Just got the word from Ottawa. I'm to go to Williams Lake in interior B.C."

"Those guys again!" I snapped. "You just get to liking a priest, then they send him somewhere else. Why can't they leave well enough alone?"

"Maybe they think a man might go stale left too long in one place."

"Pooh! Not you. You belong here. What will you do at Williams Lake? That's cattle country."

"Oh, I imagine I'll make a fair cowpoke."

"I don't like it, Father. I'm beginning to feel like the whole country's deserting me.... Slim, Cathy and Alf, and now you. I'm going to be the only one left up here."

"Oh, there's a few people around yet. Anyway, you're going to like your new priest."

"Ha! What makes you think so?"

"Well, you liked me when Father Lob left, didn't you now? So, when I leave you'll like Father Mac. I'll be bringing him around one of these days. He should be arriving most any time now."

How could he sound so cheerful? I almost hated him for it. He departed, leaving me glum and unconvinced. Even the kids' happy chatter failed to douse the gloom that had invaded those private parts of my mind.

That morning when Maureen came up from the beach her face wore a puzzled look. "Mom, there's something on the beach. I can't figure how it got there."

"What is it?"

"Looks like a float."

"Oh well," I shrugged, "maybe it broke away from one of the camps and drifted in."

"Not this one. Come have a look."

It was a float, a small one, about twelve feet by twelve, and a beauty. Almost-new planking had been nailed a-cross cedar logs. It lay half-in, half-out of the water so that a five-rung ladder attached to the float with aluminum hand rails was not damaged. Even more surprising was the huge boulder just below the water's surface. A heavy anchor chain attached to a swivel bored into the boulder connected with the center pinnings of the float.

Maureen's expression was decidedly quizzical and there was an amused quirk to her lips. "Are you sure you aren't hiding something from me, Mom? Like a gentleman friend, maybe?"

I chuckled appreciatively. "I have gentlemen friends, yes, but I don't know of one who would bring me a float—and in the middle of the night yet. Strange. I never heard a sound. Did you?"

She shook her head, then shrugged. "Well, for sure, someone meant you to have it."

The kids had already claimed ownership, climbing up on it, then sitting with their feet dangling in the water.

"Hey! Cool!" They didn't care how it got there.

I puzzled the matter all morning, but could find no answer. Then, on the afternoon high tide, Dirk Kirkwood edged his tugboat into the cove. Dirk had been an off and on visitor since my first year alone at the cove. He was the same age as Maureen, his wavy black hair a contrast to her blonde hair and grey-green eyes. His Irish grin had endeared him to me from the first. Here was a boy, I'd thought, that Wally and I would have wanted to adopt. Instead, Dirk adopted me. "Mom," I became, that very first day, and Mom I remained.

"Dirk!" I exclaimed, when he had pulled in close to shore. "I didn't think you were in the area."

"Came up a couple of weeks ago. I've been working mostly around Gold River. They gave me a run down this way today so I thought I'd pop in and keep you from getting lonesome." He nodded towards Maureen and the kids. "Guess I needn't have worried."

I laughed, then introduced him. He took Maureen's hand and held it a moment. "I've wanted to meet you since the time Mom first talked about you. I was jealous at first, until she agreed to be my Mom too. Hope you don't mind the relationship."

"Not at all," Maureen assured him. "Mom's spoken of you so often I've felt I knew you."

"Good. We're all family then." And he held out his hands to the kids. Shyly, Pam took the offered hand. Not so, Jeff.

"Are you my uncle?" he asked gravely.

"Could be," Dirk told him.

The gravity vanished as Jeff flung his arms around Dirk. "I like you. I like the float you brought us."

Dirk picked him up and gave him a hug, then turned to me. "Where do you want that float, Mom?"

I shook my head over my own stupidity. "Took Jeff to realize where that float came from. I should have guessed."

"Yah. I brought it this morning before sunup. Made plenty of racket. Thought for sure you'd come busting down."

"I didn't hear a darn thing. But, Dirk, where did you get it ... the float?"

"Oh-h, I had a little time on my hands up at Gold River. Talked some of the outfits out of the materials I needed and knocked it together for you. You should have a float in here, Mom. The airlines aren't really obliged to come into a place that doesn't have a float or a log or something they can pull up to."

I felt my face flush as I recalled my cheekiness when they'd failed to locate the cove. "I've never given it a thought," I admitted sheepishly. "Just took it for granted they'd go anywhere, no matter what."

Dirk grinned, shaking his head over what he must have considered to be the inconsistencies of female logic. "They pretty well do go anywhere," he agreed, "but we'll make it a little easier for them here, anyway. Now, where's the best spot?"

"Directly in from the islands, I think. There's water there even on the lowest tide so there won't be any danger of the float perching atop that boulder. Good protection from the wind there too."

Dirk got a line on the float and soon had it maneuvered into place. The ample chain would keep it afloat on the highest tides, with the swivel allowing it to turn with the wind. We could dive off it too, using the ladder to climb out of the water. Dirk had thought of everything.

"Brought you something else, Mom," he said as he lowered an eight foot fiberglass boat into the water and rowed it to shore. "That big rowboat of yours is too heavy to manage alone. I know you've done it up to now," he acknowledged as he saw I was about to protest, "but that doesn't mean you always have to. Besides, with the float out there, you've got to have a boat you can jump right into. When the plane comes in you've got to beat them to the float and be all set to pull them alongside."

"Good gosh, Dirk, you make me wonder how I ever managed."

He rewarded me with a laugh. "You managed all right, but this little skiff's a honey. Weighs next to nothing. It's not for rough water, of course. When you go outside, take the old rowboat. We'll tie it alongside your float. When you want to use it you can row out in the skiff. No more of this shoving and tugging."

"I'll grow fat," I protested.

His laughter rolled into the hills. "Never! Not you!"

"Dirk," I faltered, waiting for his laughter to subside, "it's so much. I don't know what to say."

He put an arm around my shoulder and gave me a hug. "No need to say anything, Mom. Just let me keep coming here."

CHAPTER 9

A Menacing Visitor

A plane taxied in.

It was August second and Greg had arrived just in time to celebrate his birthday. Maureen swept him into her arms and held him tight. Then sensing she was being too emotional, she released him and, in as matter-of-fact tones as she could manage, observed, "How tall you've grown."

"Well of course," he said, drawing himself up to his tallest. "I'm seven now."

Jeff dug a bare toe into the pebbles, pushing them around. "I wish I was seven." His voice was wistful. "Then I could ride in a seaplane all by myself, too."

"Don't you fret." I told him. "You'll have lots of chances to ride in a plane."

Though he said no more Greg was definitely the hero of the day, because he was seven, and because he had come alone in a seaplane, just he and the pilot. To Pam he was not so much a hero, but she stayed close at his heels all day. He was more fun. Jeff was too little. Poor Jeff, I thought. To be littlest is not always fun.

Greg had a lot of catching up to do in the days that followed. He had to learn to row but because he was bigger and stronger it didn't take him long. He also demanded to run the outboard. Just around the cove didn't satisfy him, so we went down to Owasitsa River. The kids dug wells in the sand and watched excitedly as the water levels rose. And one day when it rained hard, they were just as excited seeing the water level rise in the pool back of our dam.

Late one afternoon while we were at supper we heard a boat enter the cove. An Indian lad, probably in his early twenties, was wobbling uncertainly on the beach. There was no mistaking he was very drunk. It was a sad day, I thought, recalling Pat's and Vera's concern when the government decreed Indians could take their liquor out. As my glance strayed to the case of beer in the bottom of this young Indian's speedboat, I knew Pat's and Vera's decision to leave Nuchatlitz had been wise and I was thankful they had found work at Christie.

The young intruder stooped to lift the case of beer from the boat.

"Leave it there," I said.

He faced me sullenly. "Why?"

"Because I say so."

He shrugged. "Okay, if you say." But he took a bottle, drained it, then smashed it on the rocks. The clink of splintering glass infuriated me.

"Don't you do that again. We walk barefoot on the beach. One of us could get cut."

"Okay! Okay! Next bottle I won't break. Now I want to eat."

"All right. Come up to the house. I'll feed you."

Maureen had come down the steps and stood beside me. "Should you?" she whispered.

"I have to. Otherwise he'll sit here breaking more bottles and getting more and more drunk."

He wasn't hungry. I'd known he wasn't. He lit a cigarette, then slumped over the table, pushing his food around with his fork. And he leered at the kids who huddled together, their eyes wide with unasked questions.

"Ever see an Injun before?" he demanded of them. The dark brown eyes snapped. In that question was all the stored-up hurt, resentment and anger of many generations.

"Indian," I corrected him.

"No. Injun!" And in that uttered word he mimicked the slurring derogatory enunciation of the white man.

"In this house we don't say that," I told him firmly. "The Indian people here on the coast are my friends. Now, finish your meal and drink your coffee and then you must leave."

"Friend? Then why you want me to leave?"

"I want you to leave before it gets so dark you can't see where you're going."

"Don't need to see. I know where I'm going."

"Of course you do," I agreed, "but there's no light on your speedboat. You could run into a deadhead."

"You care?" The scorn in his voice, the defiant look in his eyes, told me plainer than words that he did not believe it.

"I do care." And I emphasized each word. "I told you before, your people are my friends."

"How do you know *I'm* your friend?"

"If you are *not* my friend, why did you come here?"

He studied me a moment through lowered lids, his mouth curled to the side, half snarl, half indecision. Then, abruptly, he got to his feet. "Okay. I go."

I watched without comment as, still wobbly on his feet, he went out the door and headed down the steps. I listened. No clink of glass. He'd remembered that. In a few minutes we heard the rev of his engine.

"Well, thank goodness!" Maureen pushed at her hair

though, for a change, it was properly in place.

"Why was he so mad?" Greg wanted to know. "We didn't do anything."

"No, *we* didn't, but some people have been very unkind to the Indians. It sometimes makes them suspicious of all of us."

"Mom!" It was an exclamation from Maureen. "I don't hear his outboard any more."

It was true. There wasn't a sound. It could mean only one thing. Our friend hadn't left. We weren't surprised when the door was flung open. He stood there, daring us to reject him.

"Is too dark already," he said. "I decide I stay."

"Come in then. If you want to stay tonight I'll make up a bed for you on the davenport."

He shrugged. "Don't need a bed." He turned to face the kids. "Nice kids you got. Come here. I won't hurt you. I got kids. I like kids. How old you kids?"

"I'm five," Pam volunteered.

"Pretty, too. Nice white hair."

"It's blonde," she protested indignantly.

"Okay. Blonde. Pretty."

Jeff ventured to his side. "I'm three. Pretty soon when I go back to Seattle I'll be four."

"I got a boy, four," our guest announced grandly. "I tell him stories. You kids like stories? I tell you stories."

So he told stories . . . of great warriors, great hunters, brave men who went out in their dugout canoes to capture the mighty whale, and the kids pressed close to him, enthralled. In the telling pride in his race came to the surface, erasing the curl of his lips. His soft guttural voice had charm. The straight black hair was pushed back from eyes that shone with the reflected glory of his people. Why, he was handsome! He could have been one of those warriors, and in the eyes of the kids I saw that he was. He punctuated his sentences with smoke rings or simply by blowing smoke spirals into the room as he tossed one cigarette aside and lit up another.

He had said no bed, but a bed he must have if we were ever to get the kids to sleep. I started up the stairs, a lamp in my hand, and Maureen followed me.

"Do we have to keep him?" she whispered. "I don't trust him."

"If he won't go, there's nothing we can do about it."

"Couldn't he maybe sleep in the cabin? The blankets are still there."

"No, I want him where I can watch him. I don't trust him with those cigarettes. He could set the whole forest afire."

"You're right, of course." She shook her head. "I won't sleep a wink all night."

"Probably neither of us will," I admitted. "He's had enough to drink to get really wound up. I'm sure he sneaked a few when he went down and revved his engine. We may have to listen to stories all night."

Her answer was a groan. "Mom, I thought you lived quietly and peacefully up here. So far it's been one darn thing after another."

"It does seem that way. Here, take these blankets. Let's get his bed made up and see if we can persuade him to be quiet for a while."

"I hope so. Do you realize it's nearly eleven o'clock?"

Our friend was still holding forth with his stories and the kids, sleepy-eyed and nodding, still managed to listen. But when he observed us making up a bed the words stopped abruptly and he almost sprang from his chair.

"I think I go now."

"But it's eleven o'clock," I protested. "You said you wanted to stay."

"I change my mind."

Suddenly I'd had enough. He'd accepted our hospitality; he'd disrupted our routine; he couldn't make up his mind; and I was dead tired.

"Then go!" My voice was tight with anger.

"It's dark. I can't see now."

"Then stay."

"No. I go. With a flashlight it will be okay. You come."

"All right!" And I spit out the words. "I'll go down to the beach with you."

Maureen was worried. "Shall I go with you, Mother?"

"No, it's okay."

But down on the beach I was filled with dismay. The tide had gone out leaving his boat high and dry. He tugged at it, wrestling it down over the rocks.

"It's no use," I protested. "There's not enough water in the gap for you to get through anyway."

"We push it through. You help."

So I helped. If we got the boat through the gap he wouldn't be able to get it back in, and oh, I did want him to leave. The flashlight got in the way so I laid it on the rocks. Stars lit the night, tiny beacons directing our efforts. I slipped on wet rocks and seaweed, I strained and I panted, but nothing could have persuaded me to call quits. Then it was done. The boat was through the gap. I relinquished my hold, straightened up with an effort, and sloshed out of the shallow water. It was then he lunged at me, mouthing words I couldn't understand. I felt myself falling and I twisted, trying to right myself.

"Maureen!" One shrill cry in the night.

She came running, flashlight in hand, the kids trailing behind her. "What's going on here?" she demanded. Her voice betrayed no fear. It was angry, authoritative. She was taller than our guest by a good six inches. Even in starlight she looked fierce. He eyed her speculatively, then turned.

"I go." And he shoved the boat into deeper water and started the engine.

"Are you all right, Mom?" Maureen asked.

"I'm okay. Let's get back to the house."

But as we started up the steps we heard a crash, and a cry.

"Drat!" I muttered. "It had to happen. He hit a reef." Should we help him or let him make his own way back? He was barely outside the cove. While we hesitated, the engine revved again, then screeched into high pitch, accompanied by a steady slap, slap, slap as the hull hit the water.

"Darn nut! He's going full bore."

We didn't hear the crash. I don't know why. But we heard his voice, faint and far away.

"Help . . . !" A pause, then it came again. "Help . . . ! Help . . . !"

"What'll we do, Mom?"

"We'll go in the house and go to bed."

"Mother! You can't *mean* that!"

"Oh, but I do. He's close in to shore. The cold water will sober him up in a hurry. He's young and he's strong. He'll make it to shore okay. Unless I miss my guess he'd made it to shore before he yelled."

"But he'll be wet and cold. Shouldn't we go find him?"

"No. He's got a better chance of finding us than we have of finding him."

"It seems so unfeeling."

"Take my word for it, Maureen, it isn't."

"What will he do?"

"He'll huddle up in the brush and wait for morning to find his way here. So, we'll get some sleep and be ready for him when he comes."

"Do you really think he'll come?"

"There's nowhere else he *can* go. Nuchatlitz is too far. Following the shoreline it's twice the distance by sea, and it's on another island besides."

I don't know how much either Maureen or I slept, but the kids did. It had been the most bewildering evening of their lives. Excitement had kept them going, but when it was over they collapsed, their eyes closing even before they were properly tucked in bed.

We were still at breakfast the next morning when the knock came at the door. I didn't need to look to know who it was, but even I was not prepared for his appearance. He was barefoot and pantless, but had managed to salvage his jacket. He wore it now like an apron, the sleeves wrapped around his waist and tied in the back. But it was the humiliation, the whipped-dog look, that caught and held my attention.

"Come in," I said. "There's hot coffee on the stove. Won't you join us for breakfast?"

He stood uncertainly in the doorway shifting his weight from one bare foot to another. "My boat sank," he muttered. "I take off my pants and shoes to swim. I need pants."

Maureen offered a pair of her tennis shoes, but I had given Wally's pants to Frank. Then I thought of that pairof cut-offs I'd left hanging, not because they were any good, but because I hadn't know what to do with them. They didn't properly belong in the garbage. They'd be hard to burn. But they would certainly, now, provide our unhappy friend with some insulation against this latest blow to his pride. I gave him the pants and he stepped outside to pull them on. It was with difficulty that I repressed a smile when he reappeared. With his jacket as an apron he had looked somehow pathetic. In Wally's cut-offs he simply looked ludicrous. Wally had been taller and heavier. Cut-offs that stuck him at the knees slopped down around this fellow's calves. The pants wrapped around his slender waist once and half again and he held them up, his fingers clenched in a fold.

"No good," he said.

"I'm sorry. That's all I have. But I have a big safety pin. We'll pin them tight around you."

He ate silently, drank his coffee, then asked for more. He was cold sober and thoroughly unhappy about it. I studied his morose expression and was thankful we had prepared for his coming before we'd made breakfast. The little skiff we'd stashed away in the bushes. The outboard had been removed from the rowboat and carried up to the storeroom. Oars were slid in under a bed upstairs.

"Why, Mom?" Maureen had asked.

"Because if he comes back he'll want to head for the nearest pub. I'm taking no chances on being left here without a means of escape . . . should we need one."

"You mean we'll have to keep him around?"

"Only until tomorrow. The plane will be in then and we'll ship him out."

"Tomorrow! Sounds like forever."

Tomorrow seemed a forever to our unhappy guest, too. He asked for a cigarette. I had none. Clutching his pants with one hand, not trusting the pin, he paced restlessly about the house, then down to the beach, eyeing my boat, minus motor and oars.

"I got to get out of here. I got to have a smoke. I borrow your boat."

"No. We need our boat."

"I won't hurt it. I bring it back."

Maybe . . . if he could remember after he'd been to the pub. All that mattered to him now was liquor and cigarettes. Those ridiculous cut-offs he was wearing would act as no deterrent. He suffered. It was plain to see. I felt

81

sorry for him in spite of myself, but in no way was I going to set us up for a return visit.

By mid-afternoon, tomorrow had begun to seem like a forever to all of us. The kids were restless, uncertain what to do, trying mostly to just keep out of the way. The happy warrior of the previous night was happy no more. I felt as much relief as anyone else when a small speedboat edged past my reefs and into the cove.

I recognized Cecily and Bruce from the Fish Camp near Nuchatlitz. Now and then they'd run over for aquickie visit, sometimes just long enough for a cup of coffee. Generally their faces wore anticipatory grins, sure of a welcome. Today they looked more solemn than Solomon.

"We found a sunken boat," Bruce said. "Just the rim was showing above water. Couldn't find anyone. Must have drowned."

"He didn't drown," I told them. "I have him, and you're welcome to him. Maybe you can drop him off at Nuchatlitz. They'll know what to do."

Our guest had disappeared into the bush when the boat came in, but when I yelled, assuring him he had a ride to Nuchatlitz, his reappearance was swift. Cecily and Bruce did a double-take when they saw him. Cecily bit her lip, but neither she nor Bruce cracked a smile.

"Oh! I almost forgot," Bruce said. "We brought you a salmon."

He lifted it from the bottom of the boat, and our reluctant guest climbed in. Never had I made a happier exchange.

CHAPTER 10

On Patrol

The cove was attracting visitors like flies that summer. Some came because they wanted to meet my family. Johnny Schoppel arrived towing a fir log all sawed into rolls, each stapled separately and with plenty of give onto a long nylon rope. The tide was low so Johnny left his gift on the far beach beyond the cottage. We kept a close watch. Firewood for the rest of the summer and into next summer was too great a prize to chance losing.

When the tide came back in and the fir chunks bobbed in the rising waters I went after them. With a firm grip on the trailing end of the rope I waded waist deep to avoid boulders along the shoreline, past the cottage, around the end of the cove, curving seaward again to the rise at the foot of my steps. The rolls didn't follow placidly along in a line, like baby ducks submitting to mother. They surrounded me, nudging me gently. They pushed from behind and tugged from in front. I was used to the water, fortunately, for it was a long haul and a cold one.

I had refused to let Maureen do the towing, insisting I knew the shoreline far better than she, but now I was glad for her help. We unstapled the chunks, one at a time, and attempted to roll them up the rise of the beach. Some caught in the rocks, forcing us to tip them end over end.

Each weighed upward of a hundred pounds.

"My gosh!" Maureen sank down on the rocks, too weary to even push that strand of hair from her eyes. "What a job! But you are really lucky, Mom. People always seem to be bringing you presents. No wonder you like living up here. I may as well tell you right now this isn't a one-shot vacation for us. We'll be back."

"If that's a threat I quite like it, though you may change your mind after we've slabbed and quartered all these chunks and stacked them on the upper level."

"Not a chance. You can't scare me off, Mom."

Our next visitor didn't come bearing gifts. He motored in the west entrance, circled the cove, and was heading out the east entrance by the time we'd left our supper and run to the beach. His troller was as trim a vessel as I'd seen in our area, freshly painted a soft sea-green; a pleasing contrast to the usual white and often untidy vessels that plied our waters. I was curious about the owner of such a distinctive troller.

"Hello," I called.

"Hello," came an answering call. The engine was idled and a man's head appeared in the open window of the cabin.

"Grandma!" It was Jeff. He'd tripped on the rocks. I scooped him up in my arms.

"Grandma?" came the voice from the troller. "Did he say Grandma?"

"He did," I snapped. What call did this guy have questioning my status?

"Grandma," came the voice again, slightly mocking. "I'll be back." And he sailed on out of voice range.

There was a howl of laughter from Maureen. I turned to face her. "What's so funny?" I demanded.

"You are. Your feathers are showing, Mom. You act like he'd given you the prime insult. You *are* a grandma."

"Of course I am, but he needn't have made it sound like some kind of disease."

"Oh, I don't know, Mom. I thought he sounded kinda impressed."

"Hmm!" I snorted. "Anyway, we'll probably never see the guy again."

But we did, the next day in fact. He came early in the afternoon. The tide was too low to enter the cove so he anchored out and rowed in. I watched his strong easy strokes, prepared to dislike him, but it was hard not to react favorably to the twinkle in the grey-blue eyes, to the smile that seemed sincere. When he got out of the skiff and pulled it up on the beach I saw he was above average height; maybe six feet. His hair was fair, tinged with grey. He was slim, and I would have to add trim, dressed more like a cruising tourist than a hard-working fisherman bent on making a haul. He appeared to be as curious about me as I was about him.

"You actually live here? You're not just camping out for a lark?" He wasn't too convinced it was a life I liked, but he didn't pursue the matter. At the moment he had other plans.

"I have dinner almost ready," he said. "I want you all to come. Give me another half hour. I'll toot the whistle and you can row out."

Faintly, I resented his assumption that it was all settled. Yet if he'd gone to the trouble to prepare a meal for our crowd, we could hardly refuse. If I *had* refused I would have been outvoted. The kids, Maureen too, were fascinated by the prospect of dinner aboard a troller. I was not so fascinated. The trollers I'd been on were designed to accommodate two men. The quarters were cramped and generally untidy. Fishing lines had to be tended. Eating was hit and miss. A half-filled cup of old coffee was always in evidence. The Indians, of course, crammed their entire families on board. When they ate it was bread and candy and always pop, something that didn't have to be prepared, something they could eat standing up.

I was totally unprepared for Allan's troller. The galley wasn't large but was so arranged it seemed more spacious than it actually was. The coaloil stove, the sink, the fridge were placed for the user's convenience. The table had benches on either side, long enough to accommodate all of us. Everything was tidied up, no dirty utensils were lying around, and my nose told me we were in for a treat.

There wasn't room on the table for serving dishes. We had salad first. When the salad plates were removed they were replaced with dinner plates, replete with a serving of fried rice, carrots and peas. Then came the source of that tantalizing odor we'd been sniffing: shish ke-bobs, chunks of beef interlaced on a skewer with pineapple chunks and whole mushrooms. No doubt about it, our host was an excellent cook. Even the dessert was special, a pudding containing bits of dates and nuts. Certainly it was not a meal one would expect to be eating on a troller in the middle of nowhere.

"Allan," first names come easily in bush country, "that was the most elegant meal we've had all summer, but are you sure you aren't traveling under false colours? I don't get even a suggestion of salmon odour."

He grinned. "I'd never fished until this summer. I had this boat built and thought to give it a try. I soon found out I wasn't cut out to be a fisherman. I know fish, but hauling them in is another story. I've signed on with Fisheries Patrol and I'm patrolling this area so you'll be seeing a lot of me."

"Patrolling?" Maureen questioned.

"Yes. I watch to make certain no boats are fishing off limits. I also check rivers and streams and clean out any debris, fallen logs, anything that would prevent the salmon from getting to their spawning grounds. Not as much money as in fishing, but for me it's a better deal.... Well, I'd best get these dishes washed."

We offered to help but he shooed us off the boat. "Too crowded with more than one person at the sink. We'd be standing on each other's toes. Besides, I've a slot for everything. Easier to do it myself than explain it to someone else. Have to get back to work, too. I can do the dishes as I mosey along."

Though he came in often after that he consistently refused our invitation to dinner. "You never know when I'm coming, or how long I can stay."

I didn't entirely subscribe to this excuse but he was good company. Little nagging reflections we should do our share of the entertaining I pushed to the back of my mind.

One day I came upon Jeff sitting on a boulder, staring out to sea. "What are you doing?" I asked.

"Watching for Allan," was the reply.

I left him to his watch. There wouldn't be too many more days he could watch. August, without our quite realizing how it had happened, had slipped by us. Soon they would all be leaving.

"Better let me cut the boys' hair," Allan suggested next time around. "You don't want to send them home looking like escapees from some wild animal compound."

It wasn't only their hair that had grown. They had all acquired inches. Muscles had developed. Most obvious was the golden brown of their skin, tanned almost to Indian colour, in striking contrast to their hair which had bleached almost white.

I felt pretty low the day the plane came for them but if they felt any sadness it didn't show. They were all agog at the prospect of another ride in a seaplane. Maureen didn't quite share their enthusiasm. Neither her eyes nor her lips smiled.

"Mother, what if *he* should come in again?" And I knew she was referring to our Indian visitor.

"Don't worry," I told her. "I'm sure he's had enough of us."

"Well, don't stay on too long."

Actually, I stayed on longer than usual. It was good, after the first shock of aloneness, to renew friendships with the creatures that shared my island domain. We'd caught glimpses of them all summer, but mostly they were skittering out of the way. Running feet and shouts of glee, while pleasant to my ears, were not conducive to familiarity with the wild creatures. Minniebelle hovered around again as if welcoming back an old friend. I wasn't sure she was the same Minniebelle that had greeted us when Wally and I first came to the cove. More likely, she was one of the progeny. I hadn't really wanted to know their life span. As long as there was a Minniebelle there to greet me I was content to ignore less pertinent facts.

Lulled into complacency by these friendly encounters I could have forgotten all about *him* if Allan hadn't shared Maureen's concern. "I'm taking you to Tahsis," he said. "The Mounties should be told about him."

Later Father Mac took me to Nuchatlitz and I discussed the matter with Rose. She knew that *he* had visited me, but hadn't been told the details. Even with Rose no name was used. "I am ashamed," she said, "that any of our people would want to hurt you."

"He didn't really want to hurt me, Rose. It was the drinking. It's a sickness."

"I know," she said, and there was deep sadness in her voice. "But he will not hurt you. He will be afraid to."

I felt she was right. If anything happened to me he

would be blamed. Escape from the west coast was virtually impossible. The only way out was by seaplane or boat. I recalled a happening one summer. An Indian woman had been brutally murdered. The murderer had tried to escape by sea, but had been quickly picked up. I had never seen Father Larkin so angry. I had gone with him as he went from house to house in Nuchatlitz, telling everyone the murderer had been apprehended. The murder had not taken place in Nuchatlitz but he felt all people up and down the coast should know there was no escape.

And so, after my talk with Rose, I found it easy to forget that troubled night. Allan's frequent visits occupied my time and my thinking. There were many invitations now, not only to dinner but, occasionally, to accompany him on his patrols. On one such patrol up Port Eliza Inlet we anchored the troller out and rowed in towards the mouth of the main stream that snaked into the inlet. We moved slowly, barely dipping our oars. The water was black, teeming with salmon waiting their chance to move on up stream. The plop of their bodies as they hit the water, the thud as they smacked the sides of our skiff, was a sound like popcorn in a pan, only many times magnified.

"I've never seen anything like this," I gasped.

"It's an unforgettable sight," he agreed. "It's an awesome compulsion that drives them here to their spawning ground. Take those Sockeye, for instance. They butt the gravel with their heads and their bodies, and dig holes up to eighteen inches deep to deposit their eggs. Small wonder it leaves them battered and broken. I've seen the spine exposed through the flesh. Look at that one! See the square tail? That's a Cohoe."

So he pointed them out to me, the Sockeye, the Cohoe,

the Humpbacks, the Jacks. I couldn't distinguish one from another, but he knew, and could even estimate their numbers.

We inched toward the shore, in masses of salmon. They slithered by us, under us, and around us. They leapt so high their full bodies were exposed, and so close I was sure one would land in our skiff. Many times, seated on a ledge on my outer beach, I'd watched salmon leap, but this was a new and exciting experience. Somehow we reached shore, pulled our skiff up the beach and headed upstream, clearing away fallen branches, anything that might thwart the salmon in its urge to consummate its destiny.

Some days later, when Allan asked me if I'd like to go with him to check the Zeballos River, I eagerly accepted. We set out in the early morning of a cool bright day. The Zeballos River was wide and deep, with a swift current, and did not have to be cleared of debris. We sat high on the river bank, counting salmon as they struggled against the rush of mountain water.

"Spring, or Chinook, we call them here," Allan explained. "I guess in the States you call them King. Beautiful, aren't they?"

It was all beautiful, the tumbling waters, the darting bodies and, along the shoreline, the swaying branches of alder and aspen, turned to gold by frosty September nights.

Mid-day we set out the picnic lunch Allan had provided. The fragrant odour of coffee stimulated our senses and warmed our chilled bodies. Sandwiches bulged with tender slices of beef. We finished our lunch with crisp red apples which crunched as we bit into them, and the juice ran down our chins. We wiped it away with the back of our hands and we laughed at each other.

Being with Allan was fun. It was exciting. I liked him,

oh, very much, but when he asked me to marry him I was startled. I hadn't expected it to come to this. I knew very little about him. One didn't inquire too deeply into a visitor's background knowing that the mill in Tahsis employed numbers of released prisoners eager to make a stake before returning to the city. I had come to accept visitors at face value. So, though Allan came in more frequently, and though I was certain he was not an ex-prisoner, I'd questioned him no more than anyone else who might venture into the cove.

He saw my hesitation. "You don't have to give me your answer now," he said, "but think about it, please."

I did think about it, with a happening the next day further complicating any decision. *He* came in again, my troublesome visitor. I was in the kitchen preparing my supper when I heard the roar of a speedboat. It was circling my cove, full speed, around and around. It had to be him, though how he'd managed to get another speedboat so soon I couldn't fathom. Tired of his dizzy ride, he pulled up in front of me.

"I'm hungry," he said.

"Well, you picked the right time. I was just fixing supper."

He pulled his boat up on the rocks. He made no motion to take a bottle from the boat, nor did he appear to be too unsteady on his feet. He followed me up the steps, not saying a word. In the kitchen he took the chair I indicated. I could feel his eyes on me, following my every move. I set a plate of food before him. He ate a few bites, then pushed the food around on his plate.

"I think I throw up," he said.

"Don't you dare throw up in my house," I told him.

He sat motionless, staring at me. Then, abruptly, he pushed his chair back from the table and stood up. "Okay. I go now."

He did go. I didn't follow him down to the beach but I listened for the sound of his engine, listened as he sped out of the cove, listened still as the sound became fainter and farther away. Only then did I sit down to my own meal. I understood the purpose of his visit. He was testing to see if I was afraid. He'd found that I wasn't and he was satisfied, at least for the present. I thought then of Allan. Maybe there should be a man here. But no! That wasn't a fair reason for accepting Allan's proposal.

I thought seriously about that proposal in the days that followed. I'd been attracted to Allan as to no man I'd met since Wally's death. Joy and excitement surged through me when I was with him. I could go on forever, patrolling the waters, counting salmon. But this, of course, was impossible. This was seasonal work and soon the season would be closed. What then? What would Allan expect of me? The next time he came in I asked him.

"I thought we'd live in Victoria," he said. "When my wife died a couple of years back I prepared myself to go it alone, but with you I've found joy, a new meaning in life."

"You . . . you wouldn't want to live here?" The words came in a rush.

He took a long time to answer. "I don't know how to say this. I know how much you love this place, but something about the house depresses me. I feel like an outsider looking in. I can't explain it except that here I feel I could never replace your Wally."

I nodded. "I know. I've felt it the few times you've come in. You couldn't get away fast enough. I could feel that way in Victoria."

"Maybe not. Let's give ourselves time to adjust to the idea."

"There isn't much time, Allan. I really must leave this next week. I promised Father Dee a visit. Maureen will be wondering what's keeping me too."

"I have a hunch she knows," he said.

I wrinkled my nose at him. "Be serious, Allan. Mail this letter to Father Dee for me. I should drop a note to Helen Pettersen too, and tell her I'll be staying with her a few days. She doesn't live far from the Hermitage. She and her husband used to run a grocery store at Esperanza. Since they've moved to the east side of the island I often stop over with them on my trips back and forth. Oh, better tell the airlines ... "

"Orders! Orders!" he interrupted me. "I'll mail your letters but there's no need to order a plane sent out. When you're ready I'll run you in to Tahsis." Then he grinned and some of the exuberance that was such a charming part of his make-up came to the fore. "Maybe in a week you'll have a change of heart."

I considered a change of heart that week. I had found pleasure in aloneness, but there was pleasure also in companionship. I thought of Wally and the closeness of our relationship. He had loved the cove as I did. Could I love Allan enough to give up all the cove had come to mean to me? I tried to tell myself I could, but deep down, I knew I couldn't. Part of Allan's appeal, I realized, was the simple pleasure I derived from being on the water, communing with nature. It was nature I loved more than Allan.

Allan came to take me to Tahsis, but it wasn't the usual happy excursion. Both of us were deep in our own thoughts; thoughts difficult to express.

"I won't be back next summer," Allan said finally. "I've accepted a position as first mate on an oceanographic vessel. You sure you won't change your mind?" As I shook my head he added, "If you ever do, let me know."

But I knew I never would.

CHAPTER 11

Epidemic

B ecause I was late returning to Seattle I decided not to go to Kakawis until just in time for the Christmas pageant. I expected snow in the mountains along my journey for winter had already made an appearance in Seattle. And I was right. The tortuous road from Port Alberni to Tofino was little more than a rut, heavily crusted with snow.

The hotel clerk at Tofino had known we'd be late. He was up and waiting.

"I hope you have a room," I told him. "I'm beat."

He smiled and handed me a key. Picking up my bag I headed up the stairs. I found my room, turned the key in the lock, my one thought to flop into bed. But when the door swung open I closed it quickly and retreated back down the stairs.

"I can't sleep in that room," I told the clerk. "There's already a man in the bed. Haven't you another room?"

"Oh yes, ma'm," he replied, "but you'll likely find a man in every bed. The boss just called and said a bunch of men came in from camp earlier. He filled every room. Tell you what," he added, seeing my dismay, "I'll take you home with me. My wife will put you up."

She did. They lifted their sleeping son from a cot and I

took his place, grateful for the warm depression his small body had made.

The next morning I called Christie, and Martin came for me in the speedboat. When we entered the bay my eyes focused upon a most remarkable addition. Brother O'Brien's dream had materialized. A hundred foot pier, wide enough for a car, extended out over the waters of the bay. A narrow ramp connected with a float. Martin pulled up alongside the float with a flourish, his face one big grin.

"Martin! You never told me. What a wonderful surprise!"

Negotiating that ramp was something else, however. It was wide enough to accommodate one person. There was a railing to steady one and cleats to assure one's footing, but the ramp swayed with the wind and rose and fell with the swells. Though I protested, Martin insisted I precede him.

"If I slip I'll knock us both in the chuck," I told him.

"Don't worry. I'll catch you."

I was glad he carried my bag. I hung onto the railing with both hands. The faithful old tractor stood ready at the top of the ramp. Martin secured my bag with a rope and I took a position on a small metal step at the back end of the tractor.

"Hang on," Martin advised as he swung up into the seat.

Hang on I did, grasping the back of that seat with both hands. We lurched along a roller-coaster road that was more rocks and roots than anything else, coming to an abrupt halt where the sea had cut into the point.

"We go down now," Martin warned me.

He took the bank at an angle, and when we reached the beach Martin glanced back to see if I'd survived the descent.

"Someday," he said, "we will build a bridge over that gap."

I nodded, at a loss for words. Getting to Christie was still no cinch. The fact was driven home as we forded anarrow tidal stream and drove across the sandy beach to the road that led up the hill to the school. That pier, I perceived, could only be used when the tide exposed the beach.

Father Noonan had been transferred to the Indian Residential School at Kamloops and Father Mackey had replaced him as superintendent at Christie. I liked Father Mackey at once. A contagious laugh and good humour made him right for his position here at Christie.

"Don't worry," Father Mackey told the children at the end of the pageant, "if Mrs. Flynn could get here, Santa will surely come."

Snow had come also, while I was at the school. A telephone call confirmed suspicions that the road through the mountains was blocked. But I had to be back in Seattle to celebrate Christmas with my family. I'd promised.

"We'll get you to Ucluelet," Father Mackey said, "and the Lady Rose will take you on to Port Alberni. If you don't mind, I'll send the Alberni children with you. They'd like to get home for Christmas, too."

The children numbered fourteen. It was fast getting dark as we steamed out of the almost land-locked harbor of Ucluelet, but we could make out the high banks on either side of the gap that led us into Barkley Sound. The change was dramatic as the quiet waters of the harbor gave way to the windswept Pacific Ocean funneling into the Sound.

We had been rambling around, familiarizing ourselves with the boat, but the rougher seas forced us onto a number of benches in the passenger area. A man sitting opposite me struck up a conversation. Suddenly the boat lurched to one side. My bench went along with the lurch, carrying me to the far side of the boat. Another lurch and I found myself again facing the man who had engaged me in conversation.

"It's a mite rough tonight," he observed with a grin. "Perhaps you'd better join me on my bench."

I took his suggestion. My bench was quickly claimed by several of the youngsters who responded to the abrupt shifts from one side of the boat to the other with boisterous aplomb.

In the long narrow Alberni Canal the waters were calm, but a smattering of white appeared against the blackness of our windows. It was snowing again. The kids were restless and hungry. They bought sandwiches at the tiny lunch counter, munched on candy and drank pop. It was ten p.m. when we pulled up at the dock in Port Alberni, and still snowing. I waited until every youngster had been claimed by a parent and had disappeared into the night. Then I picked up my bag and trudged up the hill to the nearest hotel, wondering at my determination to make Christie a meaningful part of my life. The comings and goings bordered always on the frantic—a needed balance, maybe, to compensate for the quiet of my own lovely cove.

The Christmas festivities with Maureen and the children were all I could have hoped for, but once the children were back in school, I returned to Christie. I found it still besieged by winter.

To coastal children snow is an incomparable delight. Only two sleds were available but this was no deterrent. Down the crusty white hills they slid, using their jackets, or even just the seat of their pants, and shouts and laughter echoed and re-echoed in the crisp clear air. The Sisters, knowing this was a sport that wouldn't last, dried out the wet garments and helped them get ready for the next onslaught of the hills.

Before long the rains returned to wash away the snow. And with the rains came one of the worst flu epidemics the school had ever experienced. By twos and threes, the children were struck down. Staff members succumbed. Father Mackey and the teaching Sisters struggled to stay on their feet but one by one they, too, capitulated to the virus. The small one-storey hospital in Tofino had room only for those most seriously ill so Christie took on the look of an emergency hospital. The overworked doctor and nurses came when they could, bringing medicine and giving instruction to those of us still on our feet.

There was little rest... temperatures to be taken, vomit to clean up, ice baths to bring down the fever, medicine to be doled out, spoon-feeding for those able to take nourishment.

Classes were kept going. As some became ill, others recovered. The Sisters taught on with no regard to grades. Sister Ruth Ann was young and exceptionally sturdy, and believed she would escape the bug. But one day it got to her too, and there was no available teacher to take her classes.

"I'll take them," I offered.

Thus far I'd felt fine. Like Sister Ruth Ann, I was confident I'd escape and it really didn't matter that I had no teaching background. I enjoyed classes that first day, enjoyed the curiosity of first and second grade pupils, and responded to their enthusiasm.

"Mrs. Flynnl!" they greeted me. "You teach us?"

"I'm going to try," I told them. "If I do anything wrong, you tell me."

This delighted them. Soft giggles accompanied their suggestions. "S'ster Ruth Ann do it this way. S'ster Ruth Ann say.... " Sister invariably became S'ster.

"Mrs. Flynn, are you a S'ster now?" Catherine asked me.

"No, I'm not."

"How come you can teach us?"

"There aren't enough Sisters to teach all the children everywhere," I explained. "In Seattle, where I live part of the time, there are people just like me who teach many of the children there."

They shook their heads, incredulous. "I think S'sters more better."

One had said it for all. Certainly the S'sters were more better than I, but I intended doing my best.

My teaching experience was short-lived, however. One afternoon when they crowded around me to hear a story and to see the pictures, I felt suddenly that I was being smothered. I resisted an impulse to push them away. They were no longer loving angels sharing their joy with a touch on the arm, but little demons pressing in on me. I felt drained. I stood up, and grabbed the desk for support, dismayed to find my legs so wobbly.

"I think that will be all for today," I said. "Class is dismissed."

There were groans of protest. "You not finish the story."

"I know. I'm sorry."

Then one, more observant than the others, asked, "You not feel well, Mrs. Flynn? I bet that flu got you. You look funny."

Depressed, angry that my body had failed me, I made my way to Sister Ruth Ann's room.

"I had to dismiss class, Sister. It caught up with me."

"I can see that. Go to your room and go to bed, and don't worry. Today I'm much better. Tomorrow I'll be back on track."

For the next nine days I hardly stirred from my room,

alternating between freezing and burning up. My stomach even rejected warm soup and my body was so wracked with coughing my insides felt raw. Several times Father Mackey suggested I go to hospital.

But I was stubborn. "No. I'll be all right." What right had I to be ill, when so many others needed attention? I railed at myself. It did no good. Daily I grew weaker.

On the ninth day Father Egan came in to see me. He was serving as missionary priest to Ahousat, Hot Spring Cove, and Opitsaht. Those villages had not been spared, either. Many were ill there.

"You look terrible," Father Egan said.

"I feel terrible," I admitted. "I think I'm going to die."

"I think you're going to the hospital, and no buts. We'll take you out on the low tide."

They wrapped me warmly and lifted me into the wobbly two-wheeled wooden cart that served all purposes. Attached to the faithful old tractor the cart now lurched down the hill from the school, crossed over the sandy beach, forded that tidal stream, struggled up the embankment and on down the rutted road to the pier. The cart swayed and creaked and bounced, every bounce sending a shudder through my body. The crisp winter wind snatched my breath and rammed it back down my throat until I thought my lungs would explode.

At the pier they lifted me from the cart and eased me down the ramp, Pat Little holding me under the arms, Father Egan at my feet.

"You will be okay, Mrs. Flynn," Pat told me. And I was glad he had deserted Nuchatlitz for Christie. His solid presence gave me assurance.

Then I was in the speedboat with Father Egan at the wheel, skimming over the water to Tofino. Up another ramp and into a waiting truck. The hospital at last! Dr. McDairmid took one look at me.

"Thank God you got here," he said.

Pneumonia! I was in an oxygen tent for four days, in hospital much longer—but Christie didn't forget me. Colorful cards came from the children, cards of their own creation.

"Get well, Mrs. Flynn."

"When are you coming back?"

"We miss you."

"We said prayers for you."

It was a happy day when I returned to Christie. It was dull and cloudy but inside that big old building there was sunshine in the smiles of the children. We had no palm leaves for Palm Sunday but cedar branches served equally well, preparing us for the Easter service.

While in hospital I'd written Dorothy Germaine at Sullivan Bay. When Wally and I flew the coast in our veterinary practice this tiny floating establishment had been a favorite stop. I had a longing to see it again.

"Come stay with us," Dorothy had written in reply. "Only Jack and I are here. You can have the little cabin to yourself and do just as you please."

Although Sullivan Bay was usually a busy place, with seaplanes and trollers coming in for fuel, with loggers, fishermen and the local Indians coming for supplies and mail, there were times when no one would come in at all. In a cabin by myself I could get the rest, the solitude I craved.

While still at hospital in Tofino I'd been visited by George and Karen Hardy whom I'd known previously at Esperanza. Their offer of a ride across Vancouver Island I gratefully accepted. The day I was to leave Christie, however, there seemed to be more than the usual commotion. Where was everyone? Where was Father Egan? No use asking where Brother O'Brien was. He was probably working on the light plant, or repairing the coaloil stove, or maybe checking the water line. And I had to get across the waters to Tofino.

Then I bumped into Martha and Moses, my Indian neighbours from Queens Cove. They had come in their troller for the Easter service and stayed on. They were dressed now for the out-of-doors.

"You wouldn't happen to be going to Tofino, would you?" I asked.

"Yes," said Moses. "We are going now. You want a ride?"

"I do."

Dressed warmly and wearing heavy rubber boots to ward off the March chill, we clomped down the bluff and along the sandy beach.

Moses was in his usual teasing mood, a most likable man. Maybe it was also because he was Rose's father that I had such a special fondness for him.

"I think those boots too heavy for you, Mrs. Flynn. You don't keep up. You want I should pack you?"

He was grinning and I grinned back. "I'll walk, thank you. I know what you'd do. You'd slip, accidentally of course, just as we come to the stream, and there I'd be, sitting in the water."

He laughed outright. "You don't trust me, eh? But you're okay except I think you look better a little fatter. When you get to Sullivan Bay you eat lots. In summer I will see if you mind what I say."

The threatening sky had shed a few stray snowflakes by the time we reached the pier. On Moses' troller everything seemed to be contained in the engine room: a two-burner coaloil plate, a tiny cupboard, a sink, a couple of bunks. I sat down on one of the bunks, watching as Martha lit the stove and set water to boiling for instant coffee.

As we sipped our coffee Martha reminisced. "Last

year when we come down, not so good. Off Estevan
Point our engine, she blow. Fire everywhere! We hardly
have time to throw our skiff in the water. Only could find
one oar. I have only a slip on so I grab a coat to put over
me. 'Hurry up, Martha,' Moses, he said. 'You want to
burn up?' 'I don't want to freeze either,' I tell him. 'You
gonna' freeze anyway,' he says." Her voice went on and
on, a soft halting monotone, no dramatization.

"We sit in our skiff and watch our boat burn to the
water and sink. Maybe another troller will come along
and pick us up, we think. Is hard to row with one oar.
Five miles off the point maybe. Only the tide carries us.
Moses, he use the oar to head us into the swells or we go
over. All the time the skiff leaks. Tin can in bottom. I
bail, all the time, all the time. No troller come. We drift
south, all day, all night, all next day. No boats. We think
maybe we can drift into Tofino. No good. Tide carry us
past. 'Moses,' I say to him, 'I think we are done for.'
Moses, he just shake his head. 'You keep bailing, woman,' he says to me."

"Then we see troller. It come closer. We are all happy
inside. We bend over so long we can hardly get straighten
up to climb on troller. My fingers all numb; curled so
tight around tin, can hardly let loose. At hospital in Tofino," she finished with a show of pride, "they tell us,
'You be white man, you be dead.' "

The end of the story was climaxed by a startling silence. The noisy throbbing of the engine had cut out.
Moses bent over it. Martha rose and reached for her coat.

"Come!" She was perfectly composed. "We go outside."

I picked up my coat and followed her. The dock offered only cold assurance. The snow formed an encircling
curtain that shut out the world of sea and mountains, and
the world of sound as well. Aware that a faulty engine

could explode, aware of reefs and sandbars lurking in the encompassing whiteness, I avoided Martha's eyes.

Staring out at the massed flakes, I became aware of a sound, a cough—then silence—then another cough. My eyes sought Martha's. A persistent thud, thud, thud brought a glimmer of a smile to her eyes.

"Is okay now. We go inside."

Looking back over my shoulder as we went through the door I observed a break in that undulating white curtain revealing the ragged coastline of Meares Island.

The clouds continued to dissipate and the trip through the mountains with George and Karen was completely enjoyable. They took me on past Port Alberni to Parksville on the east coast of Vancouver Island where I stayed the night with a long-time friend, Jean Singer. Early the next morning I took a bus to Campbell River to connect with a seaplane flight to Sullivan Bay.

Sullivan Bay, anchored to the shore at the foot of a mountain, its sparkling waters sheltered by another mountain, was a jewel amongst jewels. It hadn't changed. There was the seaplane float and the narrow boardwalk leading to a series of rafts. These rafts supported the freight shed, the Germaine's home, the combined store and post office and the cabin that would be home to me for as long as I chose to stay. An extension of the boardwalk on past my cabin led to a light plant where the curve of the island brought the boardwalk to an end.

From the moment Dorothy and Jack gathered me into their arms for a welcoming hug and a grey and white kitten rubbed against my legs, I knew this was going to be a very special time. My tiny one-room cabin with enclosed toilet and shower was no less a palace, and certainly it guaranteed less work and more freedom. Dorothy had hung colorful orange and green drapes at the windows. I kept them pulled back so the sun could brighten my room and I could watch the unerring swoop of humming birds ferreting for honey in the primroses in the hollowed logs that served as flower boxes on my raft. Even at night I kept the drapes open so stars could wink at me before the constant swaying motion of the raft lulled me to sleep.

I was soon taking part in the daily activities, catching a line as a troller docked, or the wing of a plane as it taxied alongside the seaplane float. I had an unfair advantage. I was younger than Dorothy or Jack and could run faster, and neither the store nor the radiophone demanded my attention. Thus I came to know the loggers and the fishermen who came in for mail and supplies, and the pilots who stopped for gas.

But the reserve of one group I could not break down. The local Indians, unlike my neighbours at the cove, had an almost morose solemnity. It was their way, Dorothy told me. They resisted any conversation. A camera sent them ducking out of sight. I found it hard to accept.

The highlight of each week was the arrival of the freighter. That first arrival caught me off guard. The freighter dwarfed our tiny village and the waves it set up gave our boardwalk a roller-coaster effect. Connecting chains creaked and our rafts pulled against each other. At the time I was on the seaplane float at the far end of our village. As I hurried along the boardwalk it threatened to toss me into the sea. Though I knew these rafts had withstood many such assaults I couldn't help thinking one might break loose. I hoped it wouldn't happen until I reached the safety of my own raft. I was quite happy to stay there until the cargo was unloaded and the freighter on its way, its backwash again setting our village in motion.

CHAPTER 12

Loss of a Friend

After an unusually hectic winter it was good to be back at the cove one warm spring day; good to have time to renew, in a leisurely way, my friendship with the creatures of both forest and sea, who accepted me as if I hadn't been away at all.

At the same time I was gladdened by a sign that told me I had other friends as well. A log, all cut in rolls and stacked on the first level, had shouted a welcome when first I'd arrived. I sat down on the rocks, amused at the playful antics of the sea otters who'd taken over my float. I knew what had drawn them there: sea perch, who fed on the algae and other greens that grew so profusely on the underside of the cedar pinnings. The otters resembled children at play, shoving one another into the water, scrambling back up the ladder, diving for perch, quarreling with those who sought to snatch a prize. I laughed aloud.

"Oh, you kids! You don't get along any better than some people I know."

What a picture they'd make, I thought, getting to my feet. I'd left my camera lying in the shade of a cedar nearby, having learned if I didn't have it handy I'd probably miss a shot that might never happen again.

warning. With fir chunks crackling in the stove I'd been content to remain indoors, basking in the heat that radiated to all parts of the room. Intent on a shell lady I was fashioning, I didn't even hear their steps on the porch. Then came the knock. I turned in surprise.

"Frank! Sophie!" I cried as I flung open the door. "You're wet. Come in and get dry. Whatever are you doing out on a day like this?"

As I talked I spooned instant coffee into two cups and poured in boiling water from the teakettle singing away on the stove. I kept instant coffee on hand for those guests who might not have time for regular coffee to perk, or for those who needed a quick pick-up, as Frank and Sophie did now. They hadn't answered my question but this didn't bother me. They would answer in their own good time. Still, as I hustled about getting a meal ready, I was uneasy. Something was not right. There was no chatter, which always made me feel good even though I couldn't understand it. They didn't smile and nod as they generally did. I set the food on the table and sat down with them. And I waited.

"It is good," Frank said after a time. Sophie nodded. She didn't understand the words he said, but she was always in agreement, not a modern wife, but usually a happy one. They continued to eat and I continued to wait for an explanation I knew would come. "Do you have a tape recorder?" Frank asked as he pushed his empty plate aside.

"No, Frank, I haven't." What could he want with a tape recorder?

"Too bad." He shook his head and he heaved a sigh, such a heavy sigh. In Nuchatlitz is no recorder, too. I have much to say. It will all be forgotten. Our young people take white man's ways. Some no longer speak our language. Our stories no longer have meaning. Is wrong to forget. It makes my heart heavy."

"I understand, Frank. I wish there was something I could do."

Now he looked directly at me and smiled. His smile said that there were no ill feelings towards me.

"The white man has Bible stories," he said. "Indians have Bible stories too, pretty much the same, though we did not know the Bible. Would you like to hear about our Jonah and the whale?"

So he told me the story about the men who went out in their dugout canoes to catch the great tyee salmon and the elusive whale—food and oil for all the village. Brave men they were, and as whalers, unequalled. But then the great whale became angry. Too many whales were being taken. So when the whalers came out he opened his huge mouth and swallowed them, canoe and all. The people in the villages worried. The men were not coming back. There was no food and there was no oil.

All the people came together and there was much talk. Something had to be done about the great whale. But the men were afraid to go out in their canoes. The women and children began to moan and cry because they were hungry.

Then one young man said, "I have a plan. I will fix that whale."

The people did not believe anyone could stop the great whale, but they let the young man go. He got his flint stone and a stick. He took off all his clothes and got in his canoe and when he was out in the ocean he called to the great whale.

"I am here, great whale. I am not afraid."

The great whale came and swallowed the man and his canoe. Now was the time for the plan. There were many canoes in the belly of the whale. With his flint stone and his stick the man made a fire. The fire got very hot and there was much smoke. The great whale did not like this. He opened his mouth and belched, and out came the man and his canoe.

Then the man made a treaty with the great whale. His people would take only as many whales as they needed. The great whale would swallow no more men. If he did, the young man warned him, he would come and make more fires in his belly.

"And they kept the treaty and they were friends," Frank said. "And that is the end of the story."

I couldn't help thinking of the similarity between Frank's story and that of a little wooden boy named Pinocchio. But Frank had never heard of Pinocchio. I could only conclude it was a story that had universal appeal.

"It's a good story, Frank."

"Yes, and so now we go. I come to tell you good-bye."

"Good-bye?"

'Yes. We make a long journey, my wife and I. We go to Queens Cove. Then we come here. Now we go to Friendly Cove, a long way, maybe thirty miles. Is our last trip together. Before I go I must see all my relations. I must tell them not to forget the old ways."

So Frank was telling me he was going to die and among his relatives he had included me. Why was it, I wondered, that they had accepted me so completely? Was it because I was alone; because, like them, I didn't have much in the way of worldly goods; because my house, though larger, wasn't really in much better condition than theirs? Or was it because they sensed I needed them more than they needed me? That afternoon I cried.

So I was prepared, some weeks later, when I learned that Frank's great heart had finally given out. But I was surprised to see Father Larkin. He'd come to celebrate the funeral Mass.

"I'll take you," he said.

Nuchatlitz was swarming with people. Frank was well known and liked by Indians and whites alike. They came from Esperanza, Tahsis and Zeballos. They came from the Indian villages. So many people. So much grief. I didn't know if I should intrude on Sophie but when I stopped to see Rose she said, "Sophie wants you."

I found her sitting on a chair, a great-grandchild on her lap. There were no tears in the tired eyes, but I saw heart-ache in the unsmiling lips, in the slump of the body. She slid the child from her lap and came to me. I took her in my arms and the wails came, soft and hurting, and then the words, words which Frank could no longer translate for me.

"She wants you with her," Evelyn, her granddaughter, said to me. "She wants you to sit with her at the funeral Mass."

So I went with her to the church and we sat together in the front row. The little church was packed. Many people were standing. Many couldn't get inside. Sophie didn't cry during the service but her hand clutched mine. After-wards we got into our boats, for the burial ground was across the harbour on another small island. Father Larkin spoke but briefly at graveside. He knew the Indian people would prefer to tell Frank good-bye in their own way. There were many speeches by chiefs and elders of the tribes, all interrupted by wails and moans. Young and old clung together, their swaying bodies an expression of sorrow. The words, all Indian, I didn't know, but the meaning was clear. Frank was a great man. Everybody loved Frank. He would be missed.

Then I felt a stirring, an anticipation, and I realized Sophie would speak. I was amazed at the firmness and depth of her voice. It rose and fell in sing-song rhythm, but loud and clear so everyone could hear. She was telling them that Frank was a good man, that he had been a good example to his people, that they must not forget all the things he had taught them. In the Indian way, each speech must be longer and more dramatic than the preceding speech. Sophie didn't fail her Frank. She held her audience. Their was no wailing, no moaning. But when she had finished and the plain wooden box was lowered into the grave and the first shovelful of dirt thrown over the box, the keening began anew, increasing in crescendo, reaching out to the hills. It left me weak and shaken. With the others, as in a trance, I walked down the incline to the boats.

At the village I became separated from Sophie. I wandered about, hoping to run into Father Larkin. People were leaving. Speedboat engines revved and small boats darted out into the channel. Trollers pulled away from the float. Father, never one to tarry when the job was done, would be wanting to leave, too. Where could he be? Then someone took my hand. It was Rose.

"Sophie say, 'Mrs. Flynn will stay,' " she said.

"But how will I get home?"

"I will tell Father Larkin. He will come back for you. You will come to my house to eat. Sophie is there."

Rose went off to find Father. I walked alone to the house. The small kitchen was crowded. Children darted in and out among the elders. There was noise and confusion. The funeral was over. It was time to go on to other matters. Sophie saw me at the door and came to draw me into the room.

As we passed the coaloil stove I glanced into a steaming pot. In deference to my tastes Rose had always refrained from serving me Indian food. Today it would be Indian food. What I saw in that pot could possibly be called salmon chowder, a soupy mixture of potatoes, onions and fish heads, eyes and all. It was the thought of the eyes that turned my stomach. I wanted to escape but didn't dare. I was one lone white woman amongst a crowd of Indians; the only white person invited to stay. I had a responsibility. I commanded my stomach to be still.

Rose came in and said it was time to eat. She directed me to a place at the table and Sophie sat opposite. The remaining seats were taken by the men. Without too much crowding ten could squeeze around the table. The women and children would eat last. Bowls of steaming chowder were set before us. I felt Rose's eyes on me. Would I eat this food? Did I really deserve to be one of them? I met her gaze and I smiled. I'd eat no matter what; but I avoided looking into the bowl. I dared not risk having an eye stare up at me. There was a large platter of bread on the table, and I ate of it generously, sopping each spoonful of chowder with all the bread I could cram in my mouth. The men ate rapidly, then pushed back from the table to make room for someone else. I followed their example, taking my place at the dishpan. There'd be lots of dishes to wash. Sophie smiled and nodded approval as she went out the door.

Some while later Alban came in. "Old woman say everybody come to her house."

Everybody meant just the men, Rose explained, as the men filed out the door. All of Frank's possessions would be given away. For Frank there was no need of a will. It would all be taken care of, according to custom, with no quarreling and no hard feelings.

It was quiet in Rose's kitchen now, with only the two of us left. We sat at the table waiting for Father Larkin to return.

CHAPTER 13

Cedar Bark Craft

Maureen and the children arrived for a few weeks stay.

Corky and Jan Falk had left for missionary service in Zambia and Mickey McMann, the hospital administrator at Esperanza, had replaced them as an all-around handyman at Flynns Cove. Mickey was equally adept with a saw, a sledge hammer, an axe, a screwdriver or whatever the odd job required. Along with his other duties Mickey had assumed responsibility for the management of Ferrier Bible Camp on the outer reaches of Nootka Island. And Helena, his wife, never failed to bring a picnic basket loaded with treats. Their greatest attraction, however, as far as my three grandchildren were concerned, were their five children. Kids! Fun!

"Why don't you let your kids go to camp along with mine?" he suggested to Maureen.

She shook her head. "You said eight was the minimum age. Jeff isn't six yet so he couldn't go. He'd be lonely here at the cove without Pam and Greg."

"That's easily remedied," Mickey assured her, "if you'll come along as counsellor. Helena's going with all our five. Timmy is Jeff's age—and Keith's barely walking—so I see no reason to exclude Jeff."

Ferrier was fun, I learned later from the kids. It had

been fun being with the forty kids attending camp, fun to
join in the hikes and games, fun to play on the beaches
and stuff themselves at weiner roasts. It was fun, too, to
attend Bible classes, listening to speakers who were adept
at making the stories come alive.

But all of that fun had not detracted from their
enthusiasm for Grandma's cove. The arrival of the seaplane with our weekly supplies was as exciting to them as
ever. They rowed, and cut trails, or whatever else their
imaginations dictated. They were shipwrecked. They
were pirates. They were treasure hunters searching for
Spanish doubloons maybe washed up on the shore. This
wasn't as far-fetched as it might seem, for though there
was no record of a Spanish vessel having been shipwrecked in our area, the Spaniards had indeed been here.
The inlet whose waters flowed past our cove bore the
Spanish name *Esperanza:* place of hope. Hope played a
large part in the children's improvised treasure hunts.
One could always hope, and there was always tomor-
row.Besides, they never returned empty-handed. Their
pock-
ets bulged with shiny stones and lovely, delicate shells.

"Who cares about Spanish doubloons anyway?" Greg
demanded disdainfully. "They're nothing but old gold
coins nobody uses any more."

It was quiet after Maureen and the children left for
Seattle. Too quiet! Then one day the Saveys' old dugout
rounded my islands. Sophie hadn't been over since Frank
died. I'd missed her but understood her reluctance to
come alone. Though she was active for her eighty odd
years, paddling four miles over water that could become
suddenly savage was not wise.

As the canoe came nearer I saw Sophie's
granddaughter, Evelyn, was with her. "We suppose to be
going to get cedar bark," Evelyn explained some minutes

later as we sat drinking coffee in my kitchen. "Old woman wants to make cedar baskets. I try to tell her we can't get cedar bark no more. Logging company say 'you take cedar bark there will be a big fine.' Tree doesn't die but bark doesn't grow back. Makes big scar. No good, they say. Trees have to be perfect. Old woman, she doesn't understand."

Sophie interrupted in her own tongue, emphasizing her words with exaggerated gestures, her brown eyes snapping.

"She say," Evelyn interpreted, "when Frank was young man he goes way to the top of the mountain where cedar grows tall and straight and the inner bark is tender and good to work with. Always there was bark for the Indian then."

"There still is," I said. It was an impulsive decision. "You can take the bark you need from my trees. I won't mind a few scars."

As Evelyn explained a smile eased Sophie's troubled brown face and the chocolate eyes twinkled. *That little old rascal,* I said to myself, *She knew exactly where she was going to get her bark.*

Sophie took a long-bladed knife from the dugout and we climbed the bluff at the far end of the cove, searching for a cedar that was tall and straight with the lower limbs high up. Evelyn would point and Sophie would shake her head. It had to be just right. At last we found one that pleased her. With a single deft stroke she cut a slash at the base of the trunk, not too deep, only through the inner bark, then a slash up on either side at a width she determined, about a foot wide, I judged. Using her knife she freed the bark enough to enable her to grasp it with both hands. In less time than it takes to describe it, a long strip came tumbling down around her feet and a cedary odour arose. Evelyn wanted to try the next one. She jerked and she jerked but the bark didn't come free. Sophie shook her head and pushed Evelyn aside. In a few minutes the bark strip lay at her feet.

"I do not know how she does it," Evelyn admitted ruefully.

Sophie, brown eyes critical, selected several more trees, collecting enough bark to last for years, determined to get all she could while my generosity held out.

I had thought that would be the end of our project. It proved to be only the beginning. Sophie found a fallen tree, sat down and leaned back comfortably, her fifty-foot lengths of bark gathered around her. Evelyn and I perched on top of the log to watch. Ignoring the coarse outer bark, she carefully cut just through the inner bark and gently peeled it off, taking care not to shred or tear it. It was this delicate white skin that she would use in her work. Intrigued, I reached down and touched it. It was soft and slightly damp and had a silken feel.

"I had no idea," I said. "Why, it's beautiful."

Sophie chattered happily, the old fingers working nimbly all the while. This was work she loved, and she was an expert.

"She say,"' Evelyn translated, "when she was a young wife she take the inner bark and pound it with a rock until it is so soft like cotton. Then she cut it to right size for a diaper and cuts a thin strip to tie diaper around baby. Soft inner bark soaks up a lot of wetness. When it gets too wet she throws it away and makes another." Evelyn paused to giggle. "Indians have first disposable diapers."

Sophie, enjoying our laughter, laughed too. Then she spoke again, nodding her head in emphasis, and I waited for the translation.

"She say back then Indian women never have too many babies, like now. They nurse baby until he is two years old. Never get another baby until they are through nursing. Indian babies more healthy then. Cedar bark diapers very good. Baby never gets skin rash."

"I never realized cedar bark had so many uses," I said. "I had thought it was used only for baskets."

"Now, yes," Evelyn agreed, "but back then all what they wore was made from cedar bark. It is warm and kept off the rain."

Sophie interrupted her. She was very intent now, very serious. I wondered what had brought on this sudden change. Again I had to wait for Evelyn's translation.

"Sophie wants you to have a present because you are good to give her cedar bark. She will make you a cedar bark cape like what she wore."

"Oh Sophie!" I slid down beside her and gave her a hug. 'I'd love it. I'd absolutely love it." And Evelyn didn't need to translate. The warm glow on the old face vied with the radiance of the sun's rays snaking through evergreen branches.

Sophie finished separating the inner bark from the outer bark which she discarded. She now cut one long narrow strip of inner bark and set it aside. Next she folded her strips compactly. When they were all folded she cut a length from the narrow strip she'd set aside and tied her bundle together. With the remainder of the strip she fashioned a harness. Then, with her pack secure on her back, her arms free to assist her in climbing over fallen logs, she was ready to go. Our offers to carry her load she had brushed aside. This was her bark and she trusted it to no one.

I stoked up the fire in my kitchen stove. The fragrant aroma of perking coffee and a steaming pan of pork and beans whetted our appetites. I grilled cheese sandwiches on the top of my stove and set out a plate of cookies.

"You know," I said, pausing in the process of taking another forkful of food, "I wish I could come to Nuchatlitz sometime when you're going to have a mussel bake."

"We will have a mussel bake just for you," Sophie told me through Evelyn. "Father Mac is up at Kyuquot now. When he comes down to Nuchatlitz we will tell him. 'Go bring Mrs. Flynn.' "

And in a very few days Father Mac came for that express purpose. We arrived at Nuchatlitz about mid-afternoon; too early in the day to eat mussels, I was told. I played with Lena Bethine for a while, then wandered around the village, ending up at Sophie's. Some of the cedar bark had already been split into precise widths and lengths and hung to dry in small loose bundles. Sophie showed me the knife she used. Frank had made it for her long ago. It had a rounded handle that perfectly fit her hand and a very short, very sharp blade. She cut a few strips to show me. The knife seemed to fly through the bark, the strip perfect, no ragged edges.

"How long does it take them to dry?" I asked.

"Long time," she replied through Evelyn. With that I had to be satisfied, certain in my own mind that it would be another summer before I'd get my cape.

She showed me some of her finished work, baskets woven from the tall grasses that grow near the sea and lined with cedar bark. The grass had been split and dried, and dyed in brilliant colours to work in the Indian design: the eagle, the whale, and the dugout with the brave warriors paddling out to sea. I exclaimed over a teapot encased in woven grass, on either side the eagle hovering over the whale. The teapot became mine. Sophie was presently weaving a decorative covering on an immense glass ball that had floated in onto the beach, one of many that break away from Japanese fish nets. This was to be for Max, her son. It was he who had found the ball. It would take a long time, Evelyn said, but as I watched Sophie work I didn't think it would take all that long. Her hands were much larger than mine, rough and calloused, the fingers swollen and arthritic, but she worked with a speed my eyes couldn't follow. It was like braiding hair, only many times more intricate. Abruptly, she got to her feet.

"Is time to eat," Evelyn said.

The villagers had already gathered on the beach and drift had been collected for the fire. Barefoot children ran along the beach, jumping over logs, calling to dogs that chased after them. The elders sat waiting, patience personified. The mussels, blue-black, five to seven inches long, lay stacked near by. They looked huge in comparison to the one and two-inch mussels that coated the rocks on my outer beach. Only on the outside ocean reefs did mussels grow to such a great size. Was it the greater diversity of food carried in by the sea that accounted for such a growth? Or did they grow large in self defense to resist the attack of seas that pounded them mercilessly?

Sophie had joined Lily, Felix Michael's wife. They talked for some time, after which a couple of the older boys were directed to build a fire. The fire must be hot, Rose explained, but with no leaping flames that would force the mussels open before they were thoroughly cooked. When the old ladies were satisfied the fire was right the boys were sent to fetch an old slatted metal cot which they set over the fire. Sophie placed a half dozen mussels on the slats. She stood on one side of the cot, Lily on the other. Using long poles they carefully turned the mussels, over and over, again and again.

I watched, fascinated, as steam escaped from the tightly sealed mollusks. Then, the shells popped open and rich savory juices sizzled on the hot coals. The long poles enabled Sophie and Lily to flip the hot mussels onto the hard sand, away from the fire. Rose and Evelyn and several other women were ready with towels to pick up the hot mussels and force them all the way open. A deft stroke with a sharp blade and the meat was removed. Another cut released a ligament from which the main body of the meat dangled. I was amused to see the children hold the delicate morsels by the ligaments, nibbling daintily around the edges of the meat. The stomach and internal organs comprised the greater part of the mussel and was tossed aside, to be snatched up by the dogs or by circling gulls. Sophie and Lily were busy steaming more mussels.

"Yours is next, Mrs. Flynn," Evelyn called, and she giggled, suspecting I might be having second thoughts.

I glanced at Father Mac. "Are you going to eat one?"

He grinned and nodded. "I'm game to try."

Evelyn came to me then, holding one by the ligament. Somewhat hesitantly I took it from her. I have no great fondness for shell food, probably due to my farm background in Montana where such things were unknown. Nevertheless I held it up to my mouth, but when I tried to nibble, as I'd seen the children do, it swung away from me and my teeth clicked on nothing but air. The children giggled. It had looked so easy when they'd done it but somehow they'd known I'd have trouble. I looked over at Father Mac. He wasn't having much success either. Unaware I was watching him, concentrating on that aggravating swinging morsel, he jerked his neck forward, his chin jutted out and he snapped. He had it. I couldn't resist a giggle. His face was red but the smirk he gave me was triumphant.

"Let's see you do it," he said.

"Is it good?"

"Find out for yourself. This is your party."

With him watching and making snide remarks it was even more difficult to sink my teeth in the meat as it swung above my mouth, but I managed at last, to general applause. The meat had somewhat the taste of a clam, but was richer and more reddish in colour.

As fast as Sophie and Lily could get them ready, we ate them. Father Mac and I became increasingly clever at snaring our food, and quite proud of ourselves too. The sun sank behind Mt. Eliza, becoming a deep red glow in the sky. Shadows lengthened and the fading embers of our fire gradually died out, though the smell of the smoke still lingered in the still air. Nothing remained of the mussels except a pile of broken shells. In a matter of days, I reflected, I would be returning to Seattle, but with me would go the memory of this day at Nuchatlitz.

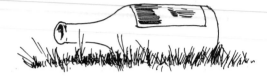

CHAPTER 14

A.A.'s at Ahouset

"Grandma, are you going to stay a little while this time?" Jeff asked me.

"I certainly am," I told him. "I hardly got to know you last summer."

"I know, cause we went to Bible Camp. Were you sad?"

"No, I wasn't sad because I knew you were having fun, but I sure missed you."

"Then why did you stay away all last winter?"

"Because I was sick and needed a rest," I told him.

My answer didn't satisfy him." We could of taken care of you."

How did one explain pneumonia to a seven year old boy? "It won't happen again," I assured him.

And so when I left for Christie in mid-November it was with a promise not to get sick, to come back for Christmas, and to spend the rest of the winter in Seattle.

On arriving at Kakawis, I was pleased to find that the indentation of the sea which cut into the point had been bridged. That certainly would facilitate our comings and goings. No more waiting for the low tide.

I had arrived in time to attend an Alcoholics Anonymous meeting at Ahousat.

"This isn't just a regular meeting," Father Mackey told me. "They have a very active group at Ahousat and results have been most gratifying. They feel it's time now to share their witness. Indian people from all over the Province have been invited. It promises to be a really memorable occasion."

He and Brother Cavanaugh and Father Egan were taking the *Ave*. Sisters Laura, Ruth Anne and Columbiere would be going, as would six boys and six girls from the senior class who would benefit from seeing what their elders had accomplished. "If you'd like to go I'm sure we can squeeze you in," he added. No way would I be left out. Knowing the Indians I couldn't imagine a meeting that wouldn't somehow evolve into a social event.

The day couldn't have been more auspicious. Wrapped in the steady glow of an autumn sun, caressed by a gentle westerly that ruffled my hair and the flowing black veils of the Sisters, the open deck of the *Ave* assumed almost magical dimensions. The forest green of the mountains melted into the blue of the sea where ducks rode the waves, diving at our approach. Seagulls shrilled overhead and a bald eagle, disturbed by the chug of our engine, deserted the tree where he had been resting and soared into the heavens in search of more privacy.

We were comfortably oblivious to the slight November chill. The senior boys and girls, with youthful exuberance, darted back and forth between the ample cabin and the outside deck. The greys and browns of the Indian sweaters the Sisters wore, the bright red jacket that had been loaned to me, and the colourful jackets of the boys and girls added splashes of colour to an otherwise blue-green world. We laughed and we sang as we cruised the twelve miles to Ahousat.

Ahousat, *Looking backward to the sea,* is located on a narrow peninsula. The slight chop gentled as we entered

Ahousat harbour. The mirror-like surface of the water in this tiny harbour reflected the many boats already tied up at the floats. We found a space for the *Ave* and then made our way up the long ramp. It was a slow process. Children hung on the railings. A constant stream of people moved, single file, both up and down the ramp. We paused again and again, to exchange greetings, to chat for a bit. There was an air of excitement and smiling faces assured us this was really a great day.

Ahousat is one of the larger west coast villages. The houses are crowded onto a strip of land not more than a city block wide. It took me no time at all to reach the outer shore and clamber down the bank to the beach. But I didn't linger, not wanting to miss any of the activity in the village. Boats were still arriving, trollers and speedboats. Seaplanes were bringing those who had come over the road from Tofino. Festivities wouldn't begin until dark, in consideration of late-comers.

But darkness comes early in November. The villagers had been entertaining visitors in their homes, but when the lights went on in the village there was a flow of people to the large community hall. Noise and confusion predominated, but gradually everyone found seats either on the wooden benches along the side walls or simply on the floor. The soft lighting provided by the light plant seemed right for the occasion. I didn't know that first speaker but there was no reticence in his speech. He was proud to stand before this assemblage, alcoholics and non-alcoholics alike, and relate his story.

"I drink, all the time. I am mean to my children. I push them around. I beat my wife. I don't go fishing. My family is hungry. Then, money is all gone. Can't buy no more drink. I decide to go fishing, but I am still drunk. I hit a reef. My boat sink. I swim and I get on a reef. I am wet. I am cold. I wish I drown. I wish I die. But I don't die. A boat comes and takes me home. They tell me about Alcoholics Anonymous. At first I don't listen. All I want is to drink. They keep talking at me and finally I listen. Is hard to stop drinking." A note of sadness crept into his voice. "I cheat. I take a little drink. No one will know, I think. My wife knows. She gets help. Now already nine months have passed. I have not had a drink. I have a new boat. I fish. My family is happy. I am happy."

Each speaker told his story in his own way, but there was a sameness about them. Each told how his family had suffered. Money that should have been spent on food was squandered on drink until he'd been persuaded to join Alcoholics Anonymous. Then what a change! Oh, there were relapses, but others who'd been through it joined forces to help. As they spoke of their final conquest their voices rose dramatically. It was a proud moment. Each speaker was rewarded by the cheers of his listeners and the clapping of hands was so intense and so prolonged it hurt the ears. This had not been so much a meeting as a celebration. In this hall happiness overflowed. I was sure that Father Egan had been the instigator of this program. Like all the young missionary priests I had come to know, he was patient and understanding, and possessed an unfailing sense of humour.

The room was hot, and stuffy with so many bodies crowded together. The benches were hard. My back ached. I'm sure others experienced a similar discomfort, yet no one made a move to leave until all had been heard and acclaimed.

Finally we rose from the benches, stretching the kinks out of our backs. The Ahousat women disappeared into another room to bring tables laden with food. For three days, they'd been busy preparing the feast: fish and meats of all kinds, stews, salads, desserts of every description, such a blend of delectable odours it was impossible to sort them out. I had never attended an Indian function where the feast hadn't been generous. This was no exception. I realized, suddenly, that it had been a long time since I'd eaten and that I was ravenously hungry. My stomach growled as I took my place in line and I wondered if I could wait my turn.

My turn never came. Sister Laura edged up to me. "We're leaving," she said.

Leaving, with all that food spread out before us? I couldn't believe I'd heard right.

"It's raining and the wind is kicking up,' she said. "Father Mackey is worried. It could get pretty rough in the channel."

Jemima, one of the Ahousat women, had heard. Distress showed plainly on her face. "You haven't eaten," she protested.

"I know," Sister Laura told her, "and we're truly sorry, but there isn't time."

My distress equaled Jemima's but I hurried from the hall with the others and ran in the rain around the houses and down that long ramp to the boat. Father Mackey had the engine running and Brother Cav was waiting to cast off. Father Egan counted us off to be certain the senior boys and girls had all returned. Except for the rain the night didn't seem too rough. I couldn't help thinking surely a few more minutes, time for a bite of something, couldn't have done any harm.

I was soon glad I'd kept my thoughts to myself. As we left the sheltered bay we were hit by a full-blown southeaster. The *Ave* bucked like a balky steer. Waves piled over the bow. White foam plastered our windows. No one spoke. No one needed to be reminded that out there in that pervading blackness were reefs that could rip us apart. We'd seen them on our way up, innocous then, but now a real danger.

"We'll have to turn back," Father Mackey said. His voice was calm but I could feel his tension. Turning the *Ave* in heavy seas and finding our way back through the gap would require both caution and skill. I knew I wasn't alone with my fears. We clung to our seats as Father Mackey teased the *Ave* into the turn. The wind and waves pushed against us. It seemed the boat would roll over. Slowly, slowly, she righted herself. Brother Cav played the spotlight along the shore. The gap! We were through it and into calmer waters again.

"Hey! I'm hungry." It came from one of the boys, almost a groan, but it broke the tension. Soon we were all laughing and talking, a gaiety tinged with relief.

Most everyone had eaten by the time we returned to the hall, but there was still quantities of food. We didn't need to be urged to partake. Jemima, her long braids swinging, sidled up to me. There was a suggestion of mischief in her eyes. "I know you will come back," she said. "I know you want to stay. I wish up this storm so you have to come back."

I grinned and gave her a hug. The children and many of the women had already left the hall. Some of the men were kneeling on the floor engaged in a game of Lahal, cheered on by onlookers who would eventually have their turn. Jemima tried to explain.

"Is played with whale bones and sticks. You watch. See. Frank has two bones. He hides them behind his back. One bone has a mark. If Joe can guess which bone has the mark he gets to hide the bones behind his back. If he don't guess right he loses one of his sticks. Each player have eight sticks. When one team lose all its sticks, other team is winner."

We watched for a while. I tried to guess which hand held the marked bone, generally without success. The bones were shifted from hand to hand, always in full view of the opponent with speed and agility. Once the hands were placed behind the back there could be no more maneuvering.

Sister Laura had more urgent matters on her mind. "That game will go on all night," she said. "It's nearly midnight. We've got to find a place to sleep." Father Egan passed by us and she caught at his coattails before he could be off on some unknown mission. "Father Egan, where are we going to sleep."

"Sleep?" His voice suggested it was an unheard-of request. "Oh yes, sleep. Well now, I don't know. With somany visitors here every house is crammed. Well... there is the back room of the church. But there's no heat. Perhaps I can rustle a few blankets."

"While you're at it rustle us a chemical toilet and a flashlight," Sister Laura enjoined.

The request was acknowledged with raised eyebrows. "A flashlight, okay, but a chemical toilet... I doubt anyone in the village has heard of such a contraption. Well, I'll do my best."

He was gone for some time and we were becoming restless. It had been a long day. More than anything we wanted sleep.

"Where is that man?" Sister Laura demanded of no one in particular.

As if on cue, Father Egan strode into the hall. "All set?" he asked. "Grab your coats and we'll make a run for it. It's plenty wet outside."

The back of the church was dark and the cold struck us. Heat in the hall had been generated by many bodies. Our few bodies wouldn't have much effect on this room.

"You did get us some blankets, I hope?" There was a doleful note in sister Columbiere's voice.

"Three was all I could manage."

"Better than none." Sister Laura managed to sound almost cheerful. "Now . . . about the chemical toilet . . . "

"You're in luck," Father Egan told her. "No one rightly knew what I was talking about but I finally found a family who had one."

Father Egan handed Sister Laura a flashlight, then led us out of the church and around to the back of the building. The flashlight made but a feeble dent in the pitchy blackness of the night but, one by one, we jumped over a shallow ditch and climbed over a pile of boards and rubble to reach our relief station. A wet night and a wet toilet seat hurried our calls. The senior boys, of course, had merely to step outside when their turn came.

When we were all safely back in our cold room Father Egan took his leave. "Good night," he said cheerfully. "Sleep tight."

We could gladly have throttled him as he left us in a cold unlighted room with hard benches lining the walls, and three blankets? If any of us slept it would be a miracle, I thought. The boys insisted they didn't need a blanket. Their jackets would keep them warm enough. So the girls spread one blanket out on the floor and lay down together. We spread the second blanket over them. That left one remaining blanket for the three Sisters and me.

I had spent other miserable nights in my flying experience with Wally, but this one rivaled any one of them. As we sat huddled together on our wooden bench, our backs supported only by the hardness of the wall, we could hear the soft rhythmic breathing of the girls and an occasional snore from the boys. We tried talking to lessen our discomfort, but the need for sleep was overpowering.

One of us would nod off, then another, falling over onto

the one sitting beside us. The blanket was yanked one way, then another. Sleep was sporadic at best, punctuated by thuds as the boys, time after time, rolled from their benches onto the floor. And of course, when one is cold and cannot sleep, the kidneys act up. I lost track of the number of times we fumbled our way out of that room and around to the back of the church. For the first time in my life I wished I'd been the son my mother had wanted and never had.

But morning came at last, and with it, Father Egan. "Well," he said, "It's nice to see you all looking so bright and cheerful. I hope you're all properly washed and ready to leave."

"That man!" Sister Laura muttered under her breath. "And where did you sleep?" she asked him, suspecting, as we all did, that he'd not had too bad a night at all.

"Oh," he replied imperturbably, "Father Mackey, Cav, and I had a good night on the *Ave*."

One could not stay provoked with Father Egan for long. His cheerfulness demanded a like response on our part, and indeed with the sun shining again, it was impossible to remain glum. We were welcomed back at Christie as heroes.

"You lived through the storm," one youngster after another told us admiringly.

CHAPTER 15

Sophie's Surprise

The following summer Maureen and the children set about persuading me to go to Ferrier Bible Camp with them. I didn't want to go, expecting a busy and noisy place. And for ten whole days! I treasured my privacy too much. But somehow grandchildren are adept at getting grandmas to change their minds.

"It's fun, Grandma," Jeff told me. "It would be funner with you though. You could sneak us some cookies out of the kitchen." He paused, thinking it over. "That would be wrong, I guess. But the cook would give you some if you asked, cause you're old. I sure get hungry." When Jeff wanted something he managed to sound pathetic and abused.

I managed to conceal a smile. They were always hungry, all three of them. How they could wolf down a meal, then ten minutes later be pleading for more would forever be a mystery to me.

In spite of certain mental reservations I agreed to go along to Ferrier. Though I had dropped in many times on the Uchuck, going along just for the ride, there had never been time to explore the beaches or the camp.

The camp, maybe twenty miles south of my cove, was situated on a point of land where Pacific waters rolled in unchecked, tumbling beach logs as if they were matchsticks. The waters rushed around the point, slipping through a narrow gap to form a quiet bay at the rear of the camp. No boat ventured near the exposed outer beaches where the force of the sea could dash it against a cliff or fling it atop a partly exposed reef. But the bay was lovely, the beach smooth and sandy, the land sloping gently to a rise where the camp buildings stood.

The strip of land, at its widest, was no more than a city block. On the ocean side the descent to the beach was abrupt, a narrow trail with numerous switchbacks. The beach was pebbly, its multi-coloured rocks tumbled and turned to a glossy finish by the restless action of the sea. It extended only a few hundred yards, cut off at either end by craggy cliffs. One could climb up and over the cliffs to another beach where the waters surged over white sand with a sucking, sizzling sound. There was an easier way to this beach along a trail winding through evergreens beyond the camp site, but climbing the cliffs was more exciting, testing one's stamina and skill.

The camp, formerly an American radar station, consisted of one large building which served as a combined kitchen and mess hall, and a number of cabins with outhouses strategically located nearby. There was a wood-burning range in the kitchen and one of the cabins boasted a small wood stove. The other cabins were heated, when necessary, with small oil burners. One larger cabin, heated by a wood stove made from an empty oil barrel, served as a gym. It was in the gym that the Bible sessions were held, and prayers recited for favourable weather so not too much wood or oil would have to be consumed.

Maureen and I didn't see much of our three children at camp. They ate and played, attended Bible sessions, and slept at night with their peers, though Jeff didn't forget the cookies or the need to remind me. The youngsters

were always under the supervision of counsellors, leaving
Maureen and me free to explore the beaches—our first
time to be really alone together. At the cove three
youngsters somehow managed to keep us both busy.

"You know, Mom," Maureen said to me one day as
we sunned on the beach, "being up here gives you a different outlook. I don't mean just here at camp. The cove
too, the whole area. There's freedom to be the person you
are—actually to be the person you never suspected you
were. Maybe it's just that you get a fresh outlook, a better perspective. Oh, I don't know, Mom." She rolled over
on her stomach, cradled her head in her arms and looked
over at me. "Maybe I don't say it too well, but you know
what I mean."

"You say it all right," I told her. "This is what I've
wanted for all of us."

"Yeah!" She paused, shifting her long body into a
more comfortable position. "Funny thing! When I was-
kid . . . well, most of the time I didn't mind you being
away. I knew that was how it had to be. But once in a
while, when you and Wally were flying all over creation. . . . "

"I know." I sighed and sat up, wrapping my arms
around my knees. "I guess I've been pretty thoughtless at
times."

"No, Mom." She sat facing me, the grey-green eyes serious. "That's not so." She jumped to her feet, stretching
her arms out to the sea. "Mom, it's glorious. Come on.
I'll race you to the cliff."

During those ten days I experienced a closeness to
Maureen I'd not felt in years. Marriage and children had
preoccupied her as my interests had preoccupied me.
Without either of us realizing it, we'd been growing
apart. Now the old closeness was restored. I felt we'd
never lose it again.

Soon after our return to the cove Maureen and the kids had to go back to Seattle, but their leaving no longer made me sad. There was a closeness that distance could not erase, and I knew they would come another summer.

Father Mac arrived one day after my family had left. "Sophie wants to see you," he said.

I knew what that meant. My cape was ready. I was so excited that when we pulled up to the float at Nuchatlitz I took time only to give Rose a quick hug before racing down the path to Sophie's house. Her face fairly glowed.

"I can't wait!" I exclaimed. "Show it to me." And Evelyn didn't need to translate.

Sophie spoke to Evelyn, who disappeared into another room. She was back in a minute, holding out a long slim package carefully wrapped in white tissue that had been saved form some previous purchase. Evelyn handed me the package and while the two of them stood by, beaming, I unwrapped it, my fingers so excited I could hardly control them. I held it up.

"Sophie! I've never seen anything so beautiful."

It was a circular cape, with an opening for the head and a tie in the front. Strips of cedar bark, no more than a quarter inch wide, had been painstakingly sewn together at three quarter inch intervals with dried beach grass. The cedar bark, darkened to a rich brown, was soft and pliable, and almost weightless. I ran my fingers along the flawlessly woven strips. They had the feel of very fine leather.

"Try it on," Evelyn urged.

The cape fit smoothly over my shoulders. I preened delightedly, but then Evelyn giggled.

"You better not to wear that in Seattle," she said. "They will think you are a heepy. That suppose to be all you wear."

I grinned at her, studying the fringe that came barely to

my hips. "Nothing under it, eh? I'll take your advice. If they didn't mistake me for a hippy, I'd most certainly be arrested for indecent exposure."

"Keeps you warm though," Evelyn assured me. "Keeps the rain off."

Sophie's warm brown eyes glowed, her lips were parted in a smile. She danced around, inspecting me from every angle, proud of her work, happy that I was pleased. The rough old fingers caressed the cape and I saw she felt it was as beautiful as anything she had ever made. Then she spoke and her words sang. Evelyn nodded and disappeared again into that other room. When she came back she carried an oddly-shaped triangular package.

"For you, she said, holding it out. "A surprise!"

"For me! Sophie! What have you been up to?" As the papers fell away I squealed my delight.

"A Chief Maquinna hat!"

I'd recognized it at once, having seen pictures of Chief Maquinna wearing a hat and cape identical to those I now wore, though his cape, in the picture, was somewhat longer than mine. Chief Maquinna had been the most famous of the Indian chiefs on Vancouver Island's west coast, admired and respected by Indian and white man alike. Undoubtedly the hat was worn by other chiefs before him, but through him it was popularized. It was a basket weave, conical, with a bell shape at the peak, distinguishing it from the straight vertical peak of the hats worn by tribal members. Interwoven into the hat, in a soft purple colour, were representations of two whaling canoes. The whalers stood poised with their harpoons, ready for a strike on the whales dead ahead of them. To be given a Chief Maquinna hat was a very special favour. Never had I thought to own one!

CHAPTER 16

"The Boat Sank"

It rained and it rained. Sophie had said it would be okay to wear my cape over my shorts, in deference to modesty, but I couldn't bring myself to subject either my cape or my hat to that open spigot in the sky. I wanted to keep them always as beautiful as the day she had given them to me.

Lengths of fir, streaked with pitch, crackled noisily in my stove. The spit of rain on the roof and the snap of burning wood with its incense-like fragrance, had a hypnotic effect. I was in a reflective mood. My years at the cove seemed to consist of a series of incidents. But then what is life, I mused, if not a series of incidents, some more meaningful than others but all indispensable in the formation of the person I had become. Those incidents had caused me some sorrow and pain, but mostly pleasure and satisfaction. I couldn't have patterned a better life.

The rains stopped at last and the August sun cast a mellow warmth interspersed with periods of damp clinging fog. I marvelled that the cove could be so serene and at the same time so alive with the creatures I'd come to love: Minniebelle, the grousemother; Tessie and Jasper, my mink; Oscar the seal; the playful otters; the hummingbirds with their strange cry; the bluejays pounding filberts against a log to release the tender kernels; the noisy crows and the screaming gulls; Reuben and Rachel and all their friends. And of course I could not ignore the chatter of the squirrels as they vied with the jays for the ripening nuts on my filbert trees. Weren't they all, as I was, enjoying these final days of summer? What a beautiful world!

One day as I walked the beach I was startled at seeing Alban and another man walking round the rocky pont. The other man, was it George Lui, or Lui George? The confusion of names often baffled me. The early missionaries, unable to pronounce their Indian names, had simply called them Frank or Amos or whatever came to mind. When these Indians married and had children, their given name became the surname for their children. So it was I counted among my friends George Frank, Anthony John, Tim Paul and many others.

I hurried to meet them, fear inexplicably gripping my heart. As we came together I could see a story of terrible tragedy on their faces. For a moment we stood without a word.

"Alban," I managed at last, "what happened?"

"Boat sank."

My fear was a knife slowly turning in my heart. Alban and Lui hadn't been alone in that boat. When Indian men went to town as many crowded on the boat as could climb aboard. And they *had* been to town. I knew because of the direction from which they had come. I was afraid to know, but I had to ask.

"Alban, who was with you?"

Numbly he shook his head. "Margaret, my sister. All her kids."

Dear God! Alban loved his sister and her family like his own. I saw his terrible hurt, his aching weariness. I despaired of adding to it but I had to know the whole story.

"Alban, they didn't all drown?"

He shook his head, in his eyes an expression such as I had never seen.

"Alban, tell me what happened."

"Foggy last night. We hit the reef off Garden Point, other side of Owasitsa River. I try, Mrs. Flynn. We swim back and forth, Lui and I. Take kids to higher reef. Margaret..." He choked on the name.

"Yes, Alban?"

"She stand on the deck, little girl in her arms, little boy hanging on to her dress. The boat go down. Suck them down too. I can't get to them, Mrs. Flynn." It was a cry of anguish. "Boat go down too fast." He paused, as if seeing it all again, then forced himself to go on. "We sit on the reef all night. Wait for it to get light. Then we swim to shore, Lui and me. Come to you for help."

He didn't need to tell me of the struggle to reach the cove. Though Owasitsa River was only about a quarter of a mile from me as the crow flies, to follow the shoreline with its numerous indentations would add a couple of miles. The reefs where the boat had sunk were on the other side of the river. It was on one of these they had sat out the long night. The five children had been left on the reef because the distance to shore was too great for them. The men hadn't been sure even they could make it and then struggle through dense brush and over ragged cliffs to my cove. They had left at first light. It was now well past noon. The children would be all right, Alban assured me. Marie, the oldest at sixteen, was a fine sensible girl. She would keep up the courage of the others until help came.

"We use your boat, Mrs. Flynn," Alban said. Though Rose called me Bethine, Alban seldom did.

"Oh, Alban, if only I still had my outboard." I had sold it to Micky McMann.

"We row."

Their clothes had dried on them but jagged tears in their clothes and dried blood on their hands and faces were eloquent testimony of the cutting edges of cliffs. I wondered. Did they have the strength to row to that reef, then back again to the cove?

"Come up to the house," I said. "I'll make you some coffee. The children will be all right a little longer."

Too spent to argue they followed me up the steps, relieved to be released from the burden of making decisions. I made coffee and sandwiches, packed some for the children and filled a couple of thermos bottles with water.

"She couldn't swim," Alban moaned as he pushed back his empty cup. I knew his inability to reach his sister was a scar time would not erase.

"You tried, Alban." How empty the words seemed! "But now we must think of the children."

Alban and Lui sat side by side in the boat, each one with an oar, rowing in unison. I ran to the farthest point of the beach where I could watch their progress towards those treacherous reefs in the distance. I wished I could have gone with them, but my presence would have been an added burden in an overcrowded boat. I watched a troller approach from Nuchatlitz and chug past CentreIsland. I saw Alban and Lui wave but the troller went on by. No one had seen. Finally I could see the rowboat no longer and I knew it would be nearing the reefs. I retraced my steps to the house. The children would be exhausted and hungry. The sandwiches I'd sent would take away only the edge of hunger. So I made up more sandwiches and set a pan of soup to simmer on the stove, then hurried to make up beds, all the while anxious to get back to the point. With so many in the boat and a westerly coming in from the sea, it would be hard rowing back, even with two men at the oars.

I need not have hurried. As I stood there on the point, scanning the waters, it seemed the ocean had been emptied of sound and movement. Then two gulls circled lazily and flew off towards Centre Island. There was no other sign of life. I went back to the house and pushed the pan of soup to the back of the stove, but I couldn't stay in the house. I had to watch for that boat.

I saw it at last, its progress achingly slow, and my heart cried out, *Don't give up. Please don't give up.*

It was three in the afternoon when the boat nudged my shores. There were no tears, but in the solemn faces of the children, in the sober brown eyes, I saw their hurt. No one said, "I'm hungry. I'm thirsty. I'm tired." They stood silent, unmoving, like little soldiers awaiting the next command.

How could I say I ached for them? They wouldn't understand. All I could offer was love, an unspoken love, hoping by my actions, by the tone of my voice, that they would feel it and be comforted. I put my arms around two of them and my words were for all. "Come. We will have something to eat. Then we will get some sleep." I didn't say it would make them feel better. It wouldn't.

Alban and Lui held back. "You, too," I said to them.

Alban shook his head. "No, Mrs. Flynn. We row to Nuchatlitz to get help."

"Sleep for an hour first. I'll wake you. Then you can go."

They nodded and followed up the steps. There was an attempt to eat, but I quickly realized sleep was more essential than food. It came quickly, a sleep of utter exhaustion. I went from one to the other. All were asleep except Marie. She had shaken her head when I suggested rest and I didn't push it. She helped clear the dishes from the table. So like her mother. Margaret had been a beautiful woman but had preferred to let someone else do the talking. For this reason I had never felt I knew her well, yet I knew she was a mother who had loved and cared for her children the best she knew how.

Marie's timid voice interrupted my thoughts. "Mrs. Flynn?"

"Yes, Marie?"

"What's to become of us, Mrs. Flynn? We've been always a family. We want to stay together. I can take care of them."

I swallowed hard over a lump that had risen in my throat. Such an old question for one so young. Already she was the little mother. What could I say? It was not in my power to decide their fate. All I could offer was hope.

"I'm sure your grandmother will take you in, Marie, and when school starts you'll all be going to Christie.

"We can still go to school?"

"Of course you can." I put my arms around the serious young girl and kissed her cheek. "Marie, you're not to worry. I want you to get some sleep now. We can't wash the dishes anyway. I have to heat more water."

She nodded and went to climb into bed with Lillian. I didn't forget my promise to Alban. When the hour was up I shook him gently, then Lui.

"I have coffee ready," I told them. "Have a cup before you go."

It was a couple of hours before they returned in Paul Smith's troller, my rowboat trailing behind. The children were still sleeping. I hated to awaken them but knew the best place for them was with their own people. The familiar sound of their own tongue would be welcome and Felix and Lily were far more able to comfort them than I.

The next day I watched the trollers pass by, slowly. I knew their grim purpose: a search for bodies. Later in the day Hank Smith and Rose's oldest son, Walter, came in their speedboat to see me. Handsome boys, both of them, their faces generally lit with smiles. Today there were no smiles.

"We found Margaret and the boy," Hank told me, "but we can't find the girl. She didn't drift up on your beach?"

"Not here in the cove. I've been all around. But I didn't go to the outside beach."

"We will look." And they sped away.

And that's where they found her, on my outside beach. I didn't have the fortitude of these people, my neighbours. The thought of that tiny body on my beach tore at my heart, and I cried for those who were gone, and for those who were left.

CHAPTER 17

"Sophie Come Home in a Box"

In those days following the drownings I couldn't seem to shake the depression that had taken hold of me.

"What's the matter with me, Minniebelle?" I demanded of my most phlegmatic friend. "There's life and there's death. Who should know better than I? Wally and I were so happy. But I've been happy since."

Minniebelle regarded me calmly from her stance in a filbert tree, her head cocked to the side as if contemplating my words. Still eyeing me, she snatched at a filbert and let it fall to the ground, right at my feet. Her aim, as usual, was unerring.

"So that's what you think of me, eh? A nut. And I believe you're right. No one should be as glum as I've been. My attitude does nothing for the children, or for me either. My apologies, little Grousemother. Those rolls Mickey sawed from that big old fir log have to be under cover before I go back to Seattle and, since you're no help. . . . " I ran down the steps, determined to make up for the time I'd wasted.

Everything I did was at the double. It was as if I was trying to outrun those memories that had so depressed me. I ran to check the dam, climbing and then descending the waterfall at breakneck speed. I ran to empty the garbage, and on the way back I ran into an old barbed wire fence the Newtons had put up to keep the deer out of their garden. A barb caught the inside of my ankle and zipped halfway around before I could stop.

"Oh rats!" I sputtered.

I bent to look. To my amazement the scratch opened, like a purse slowly unzipped, and the white fatty fascia that lies under the skin began oozing out. I watched, fascinated, as if this gentle oozing was in no way connected with me. Slowly the opening widened, and then came the blood.

"Wow!" I said. "That's more than a scratch."

It had happened so fast. The oozing had been so gentle. I'd felt neither pain nor concern, but as the blood came I realized I was going to have to do something about it. As I hurried to the house blood squished in my shoe, spilling over the side.

In the kitchen I filled a basin with water and washed the wound. The water in the basin turned red. I dumped it out and got a fresh basin of water. That, too, took on the appearance of blood. Something more drastic had to be done to check the bleeding. I hobbled to the medicine cabinet, took out a bottle of Mercurochrome, a roll of tape and several packets of gauze. Sitting on the floor, knees spread, still feeling like an outsider watching a performance, I poured Mercurochrome into the wound and wiped the outer surfaces clean. I had to force those separated sections of flesh together and make them hold. They ought to be sutured. But even if the suture material in Wally's bag hadn't been so old, I still couldn't have done it. I had begun to feel strangely woozy.

I covered the wound with layers of gauze, then taped it in such a way that the wound was pulled together. Such a lot of tape. I wound it around and around my ankle.

"There!" I surveyed the completed job critically.

"That ought to hold. Better stay off the pesky thing though until I'm darn sure the bleeding's stopped."

So I sat down on a chair and propped my foot up on another chair. It was BORING. I tried writing a letter, but what was there to say? I tried reading, but the words didn't hold me. My mind kept wandering to those tasks I must somehow get done if I intended leaving for Seattle when I'd told everyone I would.

Around five in the afternoon I heard a plane circle the house, a sure signal someone was coming in. Odd! No plane was due in for several days. Well, I'd had enough of sitting and welcomed an excuse for activity. It took me a while to hobble down to the beach. The plane had landed down the inlet towards Owasitsa and was just entering the cove when I made my appearance.

"Hi!" I called. "This is a surprise."

"Yeah. I had a few minutes to kill. I thought I'd pop in and see how you're doing," Mel called back.

He cut the engine, using the rudder to control the plane. Swinging my way, Mel caught sight of my bandage.

"Hey! You in trouble?"

"Not really. I gashed my leg a bit, but it seems to be okay."

"Are you sure? I could run you up to the hospital. I'm stopping in at Esperanza anyway."

"Well, a few stitches wouldn't hurt."

"Okay. I'll nudge up to that boulder there and we'll get you on board."

It was strange that when I needed help it always came. It didn't worry me that the house would be left unlocked. I never locked it except when I left at the end of summer, and then only because it seemed proper when I was to be away so long. I didn't worry about the fire in the stove either. It would soon burn itself out. Anyway, I'd been bored silly all day. I'd have gone in that plane regardless of circumstances.

"I need to come back out here tomorrow, Mel. I'll be leaving in a few days and there's things I have to get ready."

"I'll pick you up at Esperanza tomorrow," he promised.

A brief flight, hardly more than a take-off and landing, brought me to the seaplane float at Esperanza. I made my way up the steps of a three-story building resembling a private mansion more than a hospital, and found Dr. McLean in a jovial mood.

"Well!" he exclaimed. "What happened to you?"

"I hung myself up on that barbed wire fence," I told him with a grin. Just seeing him made me feel good.

"Hmm! Running, I'll wager. Well, hoist yourself up here on the table and let's have a look." He surveyed my bandage with a critical eye, his head tipped to one side, his lips pursed. "Couldn't have done a better job myself," he declared. "Kind of a shame to undo all your work."

Nevertheless, he went at it. I remained in a sitting position, watching as he used ether to loosen the tape. He lifted the gauze pads with meticulous care. *Good hands,* I observed, *good like Wally's.* When the last pad was removed I leaned forward, curious. Dr. McLean's bushy eyebrows drew up in an arc and he shook his head. Then he chuckled.

"Well, now! Here's something I can really get my hands into. Better than treating fake tummy aches." I knew what he meant. Indian children often had tummy aches; an excuse to leave them with someone if the parents had an excursion in mind. "Tell me," he continued, "did you faint when you did this?"

"Of course not," I scoffed. "You don't faint when you're alone."

"I suppose not," he agreed after a moment. "Well, it's going to take a few sutures, you know. That wound's a good half inch deep and goes halfway around your ankle, in case you hadn't noticed."

I remained in a sitting position, kibitzing as he injected a freezing fluid into several areas around the gash. After sterilizing the area he inserted gut into the eye of a curved suture needle.

"Sure you don't want to lie back?" he asked as he bent to take that first stitch.

"Nope! I gotta see if you're doing it right."

He grinned. "Have it your way, but when we're through here, you're going to bed. That's where I mean for you to stay for the next three days at least."

"That's impossible," I protested. "In four days I'll be on my way out of the country. I've got work to do."

"Work!" he snorted. "Work will keep, my friend. You don't seem to realize, but this is an ugly wound. If you don't behave yourself you're asking for trouble. I'll give you a penicillin injection and some antibiotic tablets to take. Be sensible now. Delay your leaving. If you don't behave, you're just asking for trouble."

"I've already told Mel to pick me up tomorrow."

"That's sheer nonsense."

"Maybe. But I'm going.'

"If you aren't the most contrary, obstinate woman! If you foul up this ankle I'll not be held responsible."

"I'll be careful."

But I also avoided telling him what work it was I was determined to get done. I simply couldn't leave those chunks of fir lying on the beach for the winter tides to steal from me. It shouldn't take me too long to get the job done. After all, I'd carried tons of wood up the bluff since I'd been at the cove. The fact that those fir chunks weighed as much as I did, some of them more, troubled me not at all. I knew how to slip my fingers under them and then lift, slow and steady, no strain. It was surprisingly easy once you'd mastered the technique.

So I returned to the cove and tackled that first chunk with confidence and a kind of exhilaraton. The things I could do! I dug a few rocks out of the way and slipped my fingers under. The roll came up, but with it came an unexpected pressure on my ankle. It gave me a bit of a shock. All these years I'd thought my arms and my back had born the brunt of the weight. I'd not given my legs any of the credit. Now I realized the burden was distributed through all parts of the body.

I sat down, studying my fir rolls thoughtfully, acknowledging the damage I could do myself. Until this moment I had regarded my wound simply as a nuisance, but now I realized there was more to it than that. I got up and counted the rolls . . . eighteen. And so I carried up six a day, with long rests in between. When it was time to leave the cove I was glad to go, for once.

And I was glad to be back in my small apartment in Seattle, glad to sit in a comfortable old rocker and rest. Dr. McLean had said the stitches should come out in ten days, two weeks at the most. I thought about getting a doctor to remove the sutures, but the only doctors I'd seen since Wally's death were on Vancouver Island. Why bother a Seattle doctor for something so essentially simple?

I'd removed many sutures from animals during those years with Wally. I still had Wally's surgical instruments. Now I could put them to use.

The angry colour that met my eye when I removed the bandages gave me concern, and there was more swelling than I felt my misbehaviour had warranted. The sutures were almost buried in the flesh.

"No point in chickening out now," I decided as I

sorted out the instruments I would need. I dipped them in alcohol, sterilized the area, then sat on the floor, positioning myself to work from the best possible angle, knees spread-eagled, the ankle drawn inward. The touch of the forceps sent a chill up my spine and induced a queasy feeling in the pit of my stomach. Nevertheless, I dug around a bit and was successful in snipping one suture.

"There!" I ignored the drops of moisture on my forehead, refused to admit my hands were not as steady as they should have been. "Nothing to it, really." And I went after the second suture.

I got it, but that did it. I fell back on the floor, breathing heavily, my arms stretched out at my sides, and I was powerless to lift them. For the first time in my life I had come near to fainting.

Gradually my mind began to function. Maureen would help me. She'd often assisted Wally. She had the guts, and I'd sooner trust her than a doctor. Her hands were gentle. At the moment that was important. So I dragged myself to the phone and called her.

"I'll be right down," she said.

She shook her head when she saw the wound. "I don't know, Mom. Knowing you, I suppose it wouldn't do any good to suggest you go to a doctor?" She grinned as I shook my head. "Well, somehow you always manage to survive. Let's see what we can do."

It was an ordeal for both of us. "I'm sorry, Mom," she kept repeating. "It's awful. They're in there so deep. You want me to leave the rest till another day?"

"No! Let's get it over with. Don't pay any attention to me."

So she went back to work, probing for those half-buried stitches.

"It's done, Mom," she said at last. "And you're going

to bed. I feel almost as sick as you look, but I think I can hold up to fix you some soup."

It was nice to be fussed over. "You stay in bed, you hear?" she ordered when she left. "I'll be down tomorrow to see how you are."

That was the slowest-healing wound I've ever had. For months it seeped foul-smelling pus. There were times when I almost gave in to the urging of friends that I see a doctor, but deep down I knew a doctor would do no more for me than I was doing for myself. He might use other medications, but mine were as good. Dr. McLean had made certain of that when I left the hospital, observing half in anger, that he undoubtedly wouldn't be seeing me again. He had given me not only antibiotic tablets, but tubes of healing ointments. I was persistent in cleaning and caring for the wound.

That winter I didn't go to Christie. At Christie one needed two good legs. Christie had become a part of a pattern and I resented a wound that was taking so long to heal. It didn't help to remind myself that if I'd obeyed Dr. McLean it would have healed much sooner. Nor could I console myself that I'd saved my firewood. Somehow, in Seattle, I couldn't attach the same importance to those fir rolls that I had at the cove.

In mid-winter a letter came from Rose. It shook me to the depths of my being. Sophie was dead. She had drowned.

"She go to Zeballos laughing and happy," Rose wrote. "She come home in a box. I lose my best friend." She went on to detail how they had decided to stay the night in Zeballos, how Sophie must have gotten up in the night, stumbled and fallen overboard.

Perhaps she hadn't drowned, I thought. The shock of that icy water could have stopped the beat of her gentle and generous heart. The waters at Zeballos were colder than in the open inlet, because the Zeballos River, rushing down from mountain heights, poured its coldness into the salt water.

There was a heaviness in my heart that seemed to weigh me down. I could think of nothing except that Sophie was gone. Never again would I see the snap of those eager brown eyes, see the smile that lit up her face as a ray of sunshine sparkles a day. Never again would I succumb to the music of her laughter and the happy chattering that filled my heart with joy.

It came to me, finally, that Sophie would not approve of my depression. Sophie had been saddened at losing Frank, but how quickly afterward she had smiled, and the smile had not been forced. She knew that where Frank had gone he was happy. To tarnish his happiness by sadness on her part was contrary to her nature. Now Sophie was with Frank. Only my reluctance to give her up was keeping her from being supremely happy. Give her up? The words were wrong. What Sophie had meant to me, the happiness we'd shared, would be with me always. Letting go of Sophie didn't mean giving her up. I thought back to the time of Wally's death, of how I'd cried. But I hadn't panicked, knowing he'd be ashamed of me if I had. And I hadn't lost Wally. His presence was everywhere, in all that I did and felt. And so I would not lose Sophie either.

In spite of my resolutions I found it hard, during those next summer months at the cove, not to anticipate Sophie coming. A small boat would round the curve of the island and my heart would leap with joy. Sophie? At times I felt her so strongly I was sure she had to be there.

One day I took a walk through the evergreens, following the trail Sophie and Evelyn and I had taken the day we went to gather cedar bark. I looked up at those scarred cedars. For a long moment I remembered many things. And then I laughed. Those pale yellow stripes were not scars. They were banners that time could not erase, living symbols of the joy that was Sophie. The cedars stood straight and tall and proud. Sophie was tiny, but she always stood tall like the cedars she loved. Sophie was here.

CHAPTER 18

"No Damn Room for Ladies"

It was a peaceful summer, once I'd accepted the loss of Sophie, peaceful even after Maureen and the kids joined me. They were familiar with the cove now. They knew what they could do and what was out-of-bounds. Still there were times when I heard the shrill rat-a-tat-tat of make-believe guns and watched three daredevil youngsters race over rocks that could so easily throw them off balance, that I sucked in my breath. Whatever would I do if one of them broke an arm or a leg!

"Oh, don't worry so, Mom," Maureen repeatedly reassured me. "Nothing's going to happen . . . a skinned knee at most. Kids are forever falling."

Jeff added his bit. "It's fun to fall, Grandma. It doesn't hurt."

And so I acquiesced, and when I went with them again to Ferrier Bible Camp I cheerfully turned them over to their counsellors, delighting in uncluttered times with Maureen.

When we returned to the cove Father Mac, with a little prodding, took us to Nuchatlitz. He'd been reluctant to do so, as had Father Larkin before him. Not enough life jackets, they'd intimated. Or maybe they had thought it best to wait for the Indians to take the initiative, bringing their children first to visit us. But Rose and Alban had visited any number of times, bringing their youngsters. Martha and Moses had come from Queens Cove, with them the five children they'd taken in when the parents drowned. Greg and Pam and Jeff didn't think of these children as Indians. They were just kids that lived near Grandma and came over sometimes.

So this time when Father Mac gave me his worn-out excuse I protested. "Come on, Father Mac. You'll have to come up with some better reason than that. I have life jackets to spare for all of us."

He grinned and agreed to take us admitting, a bit sheepishly, he'd not wanted to take responsibility for our safety in waters that could be placid one moment, rambunctious the next.

"I'll share the responsibility," I assured him. "Rose has asked us over so many times. The kids want to go."

And they loved it. With the other kids they munched berries picked in the brush. They ran in and out of thehouse, hoping for handouts: a slice of Rose's good homemade bread spread with jelly or peanut butter. My Lena Bethine was growing taller and slimmer. She ate her share and followed along on little legs that somehow managed to keep up. They all romped with the family dog and her puppies.

It was while Rose and I were having coffee that one of the puppies choked and pawed at his mouth, squealing in fright. Lena Bethine had come into the kitchen.

"Oh," she cried, picking up the struggling pup. "My puppy die?"

"Let me see him," I said. I forced his mouth open and dug out a moist wad of pancakes.

"Don't give puppy any more of your pancakes, Lena. He is too little. He can't swallow them."

"Oh, poor puppy," she crooned, taking him in her

arms. "You okay now?" Reassured he was, her tone changed. "You bad puppy. You don't beg no more my pancakes." Then she hugged him and ran off to play.

"My family is growing up," Rose said. She smiled contentedly. Then she added, "It is good how our children play together."

Father Mac was finally convinced that although my three were city kids they weren't going to do anything foolish like falling overboard. He had always been a favourite visitor at the cove and now Nuchatlitz became our favourite place for an excursion. Father Mac had retained the same shyness I'd observed when Father Larkin had first introduced him, but he never held himself apart from the children's games even though they sometimes made him feel silly. It wasn't hard to spot his discomfiture. The colour rose easily in his cheeks, but he laughed with the rest of us, his laughter as fresh and contagious as a schoolboy's.

Soon after Maureen and the children returned to Seattle he told me he would be moving on to a new assignment. Though I'd come to accept the fact that each priest's stay on the coast was relatively short, the goodbyes were difficult. In our sparsely settled area it didn't take long to become close friends. He didn't leave, however, until he'd brought out his replacement, Father Gerry.

Father Gerry was shorter and stockier than Father Mac, but the real difference lay in his attitudes. He was open and friendly and easy to know. In a way he was like Father Larkin, but without Father Larkin's dependability. If Father Larkin told me he'd visit me on a certain day I knew he would, regardless of weather or any other unforeseen circumstance. With Father Gerry, I quickly learned, it was a matter of not expecting him until I saw him.

"Father Gerry," I protested one day, "*where* have you been? You said you'd be in on Monday. It's Friday. I've been worried."

His answer was a laugh. Whether it was to ease his conscience or to put me off so I'd forget to scold I was never able to determine. However, it worked. No one could resist that laugh. It was as spontaneous as a summer breeze and as joyful as a stream rippling over the rocks.

"Don't you think I'm big enough to take care of myself?" he asked.

"You are," I admitted, sizing him up. "But where *have* you been?"

He laughed again. "You women and your one-track minds. There were a lot more families to visit at Kyuquot than I figured. You get to singing and playing the guitar, and time loses its meaning."

He could out-Indian the Indians. If he felt like lingering at Kyuquot and was late reaching Nuchatlitz, it was immaterial. If, on his travels, he decided on an unscheduled stop, he made it. Because of his penchant for keeping us all dangling he soon acquired a nickname: Father E . . . Eventually! But no matter how provoked we got, when he did show up he was promptly forgiven. No one could resist his unfailing good humour, his hearty laugh and the guitar that went everywhere with him.

One warm September day when I was thinking Father E might possibly come in, someone else came instead. I'd put off asking the airlines to pick me up, finding it more difficult each year to persuade myself it was time to leave. I'd stay as long as the weather held, I'd decide, and then I'd extend my stay because the weather was too stormy to think of going anywhere. I was still making excuses the day Bruce roared in with his speedboat. He was in one gosh-awful hurry.

"Can you come over?" he pleaded. "The *Packer*'s due in Saturday. I've got to have the camp closed up, the salmon crated, the inventory taken; and be ready to move out. Cecily's sick. I'm in a bind."

"What's wrong with her?" I asked.

He pushed an impatient hand through a mass of tousled brown hair. "Darned if I know. She just lays in bed and cries."

"Doesn't sound like Cecily. Okay, but you'll have to help me get the house in order, and you'll have to make some arrangements for me to get out of the country. It's time I left too."

"No sweat about that," he assured me. "You can go out on the *Packer* with us."

"You sure?"

"Sure I'm sure. The captain's a good guy."

So we closed up the house and I went to the fish camp with Bruce. Later that day Father E stopped in. It didn't matter to him that Cecily and Bruce weren't Catholic and certainly his status as priest left them singularly unabashed. He strummed old folk songs on his guitar and we all joined in the singing, even Cecily.

"So you're leaving our fair country," Father Gerry said after a second round of songs and innumerable cups of coffee. "I'll be going down to Tofino myself in a few days. You can ride along with me if you like."

I pondered the invitation. Seventy to eighty miles on the open sea in his twenty-six foot speedboat would be an experience. "What day will you be leaving?" I asked.

He shrugged. "Oh, I don't know. I have a few things to do first."

I should have guessed, I thought. Cecily and Bruce would leave Saturday. I could find myself holding fort at the camp alone. Still, I was tempted, until I caught the expression in Cecily's eyes and the tears close to the surface. *What is the matter with her?* I wondered.

"Another time maybe, Father Gerry."

The camp, on its base of floating cedar logs and surrounded by tiny islands, had the feel of seclusion. Weighed down now by thousands of pounds of salmon, it sat low in the water. The decking seemed always to be wet. The building, probably no more than twenty by sixty feet, gave over half its space to the ice house. The remainder was divided between a weighing-in platform, a cramped store, and a two-by-four kitchen, bedroom and a cubbyhole for a toilet and shower stall.

The kitchen could be described as convenient. The table sat snug against the outer wall and the store wall. A third of the table space was reserved for the radiophone. We could hardly begrudge the space it usurped. We sat close together, elbows colliding as we used our knives and forks. From the table we could reach to the stove for a pan of vegetables or into the refrigerator for a carton of milk.

Sometimes when Cecily had visited me at the cove she had lamented the confinement. "It's like serving out a sentence. There you are, and there you sit... until the close of the fishing season."

In spite of the confinement, in spite of the stench of salmon and the slime that could send one skidding across the decking, and in spite of a lot of hard work, I enjoyed my time there, thrilling to an ice house groaning with salmon, loving the feel of the sea in its varying moods. I was quite happy, even with Cecily lying in bed a good share of the time... until that early Saturday morning when the *Packer* arrived. I stood confidently beside Bruce as he requested I be allowed to go out with them. Steel blue eyes bored into me, reducing me to the dubious status of a freeloader. As captain of the *Packer*, the man with the blue eyes had an unqualified advantage.

"This is no damn cruise ship," he growled. "She's a work boat." He ignored me, addressing himself to Bruce. "You and Cecily . . . okay, but there's no damn room for ladies."

"Mrs. Flynn is no lady," Bruce defended me. "She lives by herself and chops her own wood. Hell! She'sworked like a dog these last three days. I couldn't have
closed camp without her. Cecily's sick."

"Humph!" the Captain snorted, and he turned, the whole hulking six feet of him, and stomped off.

In my worn, torn jeans I looked more tramp than lady, not that it mattered. I looked like any other west-coaster. I wasn't ashamed of my appearance but the raw scorn in the captain's voice had effectively squashed my ego. With downcast eyes I followed the movement of a jellyfish propelling itself along, feeling a peculiar kinship to that flaccid creature. Then Bruce's hand was on my arm.

"Still work to do."

"Bruce," I said as we stepped into the store, "If you haven't disconnected that radiophone, you'd better see if you can get me a seaplane."

"What for?"

"Well!" My voice rose a pitch. "It's not likely I'll be going out on the *Packer* and I have no intention of sitting in the bush all winter either. I should have gone with Father E."

"There's no reason you can't go out on the *Packer*."

"No reason!"

"Well, he didn't say no."

"And he certainly didn't say yes," I snapped.

"Don't get all up-tight. The Captain's really a good guy when you get to know him. Anyway, if he didn't say no, he means yes."

"He has a queer way of saying yes. I don't fancy being holed up with him for two days and two nights, that's for sure."

Soft crying from the next room interrupted me. "Are you all right, Cecily," I called.

She was lying on the bed, her slender body shaking. "I was sure you'd go out with us," she managed between sobs.

"But Cecily, the Captain said quite clearly there's no room."

"So what?" Bruce broke in. "there's no room for you here either, but we've managed."

That much I had to concede. Bruce had set up a folding cot and I'd slept between bags of potatoes on the one side and a conglomeration of fishing gear on the other. And I'd slept well, if not long. Fishermen are up at the crack of dawn. A pounding on the door that first morning had awakened me and Bruce, in his bathrobe, had stumbled sleepily to turn the key in the lock. I'd scrunched under my blanket as I responded to the fisherman's cheery, "Good morning, Mrs. Flynn." But that early caller, and the others who followed, had no real interest in me. They were after those last fish. They had selected needed items and disappeared into the morning greyness. We'd heard the throbbing of engines as, one by one, the trollers had pulled away from the float.

"I'm sorry, Cecily . . . " I got no further. Cecily was crying . . . uncontrollably.

"Oh-aa-aww! I feel terrible. I think maybe I'm pregnant."

"Cecily, why didn't you say so before?"

"Because I don't know. Why couldn't I have waited till I could see a doctor? I'm just stu-u-pid!" she ended in a wail.

The nausea of my own pregnancy, though many years ago, was not forgotten. Under normal conditions it could be a trying experience. Add to it the movement of the sea and the stench of salmon and the effect could be devastating.

"Cecily, quit crying now. We'll all go out on the *Packer*." I caught Bruce's grin and could gladly have shaken his teeth out. It was a conspiracy, no less.

Dismantling the camp took the full day. By evening the crates of salmon were stacked deep in the belly of the *Packer* and the camp paraphernalia stowed away in the hold. I clambered aboard unassisted. And there I stood smarting under the stigma of the unwanted.

The odour of coffee and roast beef wafting up from the galley brought the saliva to my mouth. My stomach gurgled.

"Come on," Cecily urged, tugging at my arm. "Let's go down."

Bruce intervened. "Not yet. The crew's having supper. We're not guests, you know. We have to wait our turn. Let's walk around the deck and get the feel of the ship."

The sea was calm and I relaxed to the ship's gentle roll. After the pungent odour of fish at camp, the salt air was refreshing. A light breeze caressed my cheeks. Seagulls circled overhead, diving, soaring, waiting for tidbits. Cecily, Bruce and I walked the deck in silence, staring at the dusky outlines of precipitous cliffs and crags that sounded the death knell for many an unwary ship. The graveyard of the Pacific, we called this forbidding stretch of Vancouver Island. Softened by the gathering dusk, however, it didn't seem so terrible.

Bruce broke the silence. "Kind of makes you hate to leave. This country really gets to you." I nodded agreement. "Who'll be up first next summer?" he challenged me. "You or me?"

"We'll see!"

But Cecily was restless. "Come to the Hoo-Hoo with me," she said, linking her arm through mine.

"The Hoo-Hoo?" I looked at Bruce. He just stood there grinning so I walked back along the deck with Cecily. Stepping over a doorsill, we looked down the steps into the galley. The men were still at the table. My empty stomach did a flip-flop. Cecily proceeded through an open doorway into a cubby hole containing a sink and a mirror. Opposite the open doorway was a closed door. She opened it, revealing a toilet and a galvanized bucket attached to a long rope. Another door opened to the starboard deck.

"Hoo-Hoo!" I gasped.

She gave me a little push. "I'll show you how it works. We drop the bucket over the side of the ship and fill it with water. We have to be careful though. With the boat moving forward and a full pail dragging back, we could be pulled overboard. See the bilge water running out of that hole?"

I nodded, careful not to lean over too far, not liking the thought of a dip in the Pacific at the end of a rope, or any other way. Cecily was lowering the bucket.

"See?" And she hauled up a full bucket. "To flush the toilet," she explained as she closed both doors, setting the bucket against one of them. "Lean against the other door," she directed. "There's no locks."

"Great! I suppose that's why you call this the Hoo-Hoo, or is it the Who-Who? Who the hell's in there?"

Cecily giggled. Away from the overpowering odour of salmon she was feeling better. She picked up the bucket and poured the water into the toilet bowl. There was the familiar flushing sound. I moved away from my door and it swung inward. Bruce was standing at the top of the steps leading to the galley.

"Hurry it up, you two! Our supper's ready."

We washed at the little sink and followed him down the steps. The cook's round face wore a broad grin of welcome. I began to feel better.

"Good and hungry, I'll bet," he greeted us. "Food's coming right up." On each plate he put a baked potato, a generous serving of roast beef and a heaping mound of corn. On a smaller plate went a serving of salad. The cook poured mugs of steaming black coffee and sat down with us. He smiled as I dipped my fork into the food.

"Mmm!" I mumbled. "Everything tastes so good."

His face lit up, but then he frowned. "What's wrong with you, young one?" he demanded of Cecily. "Something you don't like?"

She shook her head, eyes downcast. "I'm just not hungry."

"She hasn't been feeling well," Bruce hastened to explain, gulping coffee.

But the cook was insistent. "Better you eat a little something. Some soup, maybe?"

Again she shook her head. "No, thank you. I just don't feel like eating."

"Take your time. Eat what you can."

I sympathized. If, indeed, she was pregnant, even the smell of food could be nauseating. Bruce surreptitiously scooped some of her food onto his plate and was still able to enjoy the second helpings the cook dished up. Cecily nodded towards the steps as I finished and I got up and followed her. Her lower lip was trembling. "I think I'm going to heave," she whispered as we entered the Hoo-Hoo.

She heaved and I hauled up the bucket of water, lucky in my first try. Bruce was drying dishes when we returned to the galley. There seemed to be a continuous run on coffee. Each man had his own mug, hung on a peg over the sink. He'd fill his mug from the huge pot steaming on the stove, gulp the coffee, then rinse the mug and re-hang it before disappearing back to the mysterious duties that claimed him. I found it all most pleasant, but it was late and there were dark circles under Cecily's eyes.

"Don't you think you should get her to bed somewhere, Bruce?"

He nodded, running anxious fingers through his hair. "I don't know where though. Coming up we slept in a little hole up in the bow, but it's awfully damp. It's not too good for her the way she is now."

The Captain was coming down the steps, the first I'd seen of him since coming aboard. He pulled off his cap, swung a long leg over the bench and sat down facing me. A slight smile eased the firm line of his mouth.

"I couldn't help overhearing," he said. "Why don't you kids sleep here in the galley? It'll be noisy with the men coming in for coffee and changing shift every four hours, but it'll be warm and dry."

A look of relief spread over Bruce's face. "Gosh, thanks," he said. "Cecily sure doesn't feel good. I'll fix your bed under the oven door, Honey. You'll be nice and cozy there."

The Captain nodded approval. "Good idea. We keep it open for heat anyway." Then his gaze fell on me. I winced inwardly, but met his eyes squarely. Would I end up in the hold perhaps? "You're not so big," he said. "You'll fit under the table. I'll warn the men."

His eyes were twinkling. Why, he really was nice. "Don't worry," I assured him. "Once I'm asleep it will take a lot to disturb me."

He laughed, finished his coffee and climbed the steps.

Bruce had laid out a sleeping bag for Cecily and was trying to comfort her.

"It's so hard, no matter which way I turn," she fretted.

"Put the other sleeping bag under her," I suggested. "It will serve as a mattress."

"If you'd rather," the cook offered, "one of you can use my bunk."

"I'm okay now," Cecily declared.

He shrugged, scratching the bald spot on his head as he pushed the curtain aside. I could see the crew's quarters were not much more than a cubby hole either, room for four bunks, one above, one below on either side, and very little space between. The cook yanked a couple of blankets off the bunks and handed them to Bruce.

"I'll be off then. Have to leave one light on in here, but I'll turn the others off. Help yourself to coffee or anything you want."

Bruce was on his hands and knees smoothing out a blanket under the table. "Okay, my lady, lie down and I'll cover you up."

As he spread the other blanket over me he hesitated a moment, then leaned over and kissed me on the cheek. And I was glad I'd come along even though there was no damn room for ladies. It had been a long day. I was a-sleep almost immediately.

Morning found us stiff and lame, sticky in the clothing which we had worn all the night. I groaned as I rolled out from under the table. The crew was coming down for breakfast. I met the Captain on the steps.

"How did you sleep?" There was a glint of amusement in the blue eyes.

I didn't bat an eye. "Fine," I replied.

With Cecily I visited the Hoo-Hoo and splashed cold water on my face at the sink. Then we sat out on deck, awaiting our breakfast call. The brisk salt air snatched the sleep from our eyes and we began to feel better.

As the day progressed the sea kicked up. Cecily howled openly. The men stared, bewildered. Bruce wore a helpless expression. A pregnant wife, even a maybe pregnant wife, he hadn't counted on. Cecily and I made countless trips to the Hoo-Hoo and I became expert with the bucket. Late afternoon we reached Ucluelet. The camp here was more elaborate, set on a raft with a long ramp extending to shore.

"You girls may as well go ashore," the Captain suggested. "We'll be here the rest of the day and probably all night."

I was in no hurry to comply. With the weight of the Captain's disapproval lifted I could enjoy watching their work. I marveled at the numbers of crates the crane lifted from the camp deck and lowered into the hold. When the crates were stowed away, the *Packer* took on more ice. The crew shovelled, covering the crates of salmon with fresh ice.

"I wonder," I said later as Cecily and I strolled along the village streets, "if people know how much is involved in getting their fish to market?"

"They probably couldn't care less, as long as they get it."

We did stay overnight at Ucluelet. Our progress next day was slowed by fog in the Alberni Canal, but early in the afternoon we pulled up alongside the pier at Port Alberni. For the crew of the *Packer* it was the end of the line.

"Let's stay in Port Alberni tonight," Bruce suggested. "We'll go to the best hotel, get a couple of nice rooms with good soft beds and really live it up."

"I just want to get out of these clothes." Cecily

squirmed uncomfortably. "I feel like I'm glued into them."

We got our rooms and after I had bathed and rested I rang their room. Bruce answered.

"Ready to eat?" I asked.

"Not yet. Cecily's in the tub."

"In the tub? It's been hours."

"I know. This is her third bath. She says she still smells like a salmon."

CHAPTER 19

Chief Dan at Christie

June 20th, 1971, began a three day period those of us who have lived on Vancouver Island's west coast will never forget. After seventy-one years of guiding children from the first through the eighth grades, Christie School was closing its doors. The government had decreed that Indian children must be integrated. A new school, and a boarding hostel for the Indian children, was being built at Tofino. There were mixed feelings regarding the change. The often-heard, "Maybe it will be okay," was more question than statement. Would first graders, with little or no exposure to the white man's ways and only a minimal understanding of the English language, be able to keep pace with the more aggressive and knowledgeable white children? Since Christie had opened its doors on May 29th, 1900, some 8000 boys and girls from remote Indian villages had come here to learn to read and write and speak the English language.

We loved that old building, all of us. In the new hostel only two children would be assigned to each tiny roomette. The children, without a doubt, would miss the crowded dormitories at Christie where happy voices called out in the darkness, where irrepressible giggles were smothered under the covers. At Christie they helped

with the chores as they did at home; preparing vegetables, washing dishes, cleaning, helping out in the
laundry and the carpenter shop and in general maintenance work.

Old Edith Simon shook her head gravely. Eighty-four
years old, she was Christie's oldest living graduate. "Old
school is best," she said. "No work at new school. Is not
good for children to be spoiled by not enough work to
do."

In spite of the doubts, an almost carnival spirit seemed
to prevail at Christie. Programs were put on by the children. There were the graduation exercises for the eighth
graders. There were speeches, and each village performed
its own special native dance. Down on the beach baseball
and tug-of-war enthusiasts vied for space.

During the three days of the closing ceremonies over
1000 people must have wandered down the long corri-
dors of the old school. All the priests I had known during
my years on the coast had returned for the occasion.

Early morning of the first day Sister Laura took me
aside. "How about being our official greeter? You know
most everyone. With the children involved in so many
programs we Sisters simply haven't time to look after
guests. If you see anyone looking lost or lonely, take them
under your wing. Two of the older Benedictine Sisters are
coming from Mount Angel in Oregon. They'll want to be
shown around. There's been a lot of changes since they
were here. Then there's Chief Dan George from North
Vancouver. He's been on TV and was in that movie,
LITTLE BIG MAN, but he's really rather shy. His room's
right across the hall from yours. And, oh, if you could
help the children with their costumes..." She paused
and laughed. "I hope you'll find time to eat."

"Don't worry. I'm not one to go hungry." And then I
added, "I'm going to enjoy this assignment."

"I rather thought you would. Well, have fun. We'll bump into each other occasionally." And with that she rushed off.

I did have fun. I escorted the Benedictine Sisters for a while but it soon became apparent they'd rather be on their own. They were continually stopping to greet someone.

"You look familiar," they'd say. "What is your name?" And then, "Oh, I knew your mother." Or maybe it was their father or their grandparents. So the conversation was launched and would go on until they spotted another familiar face.

With Chief Dan George it was another story. The door to his room remained tightly closed, in contrast to mine, which was always open. My room, though small, offered a sanctuary of sorts to young mothers and their babies. The mothers were girls I had watched grow up here at Christie. Now they were back, proud to show me their babies.

I loved all these young mothers. Most of them had gone to the cities after graduation, where they could find work, and where they had found husbands. How nice they all looked, as fashionable as any young matron in Vancouver! They liked pretty clothes for themselves and for their babies. The babies with their black hair, their round brown faces and serious chocolate eyes, resembled a collection of dolls. On those occasions when I could stop by my room there were always so many to greet me. There was no time to wonder about Chief Dan's closed door.

Around noon that first day I went down to the Priests' dining room. I'd often shared their meals and felt certain if there wasn't room for me they'd make room. As I joined them I thought to myself that missionary priests never grow up. Their hair had thinned maybe just a bit, or had become flecked with grey, but their abounding good humour was unaffected by the years. They were inveterate teasers and anyone was fair game. I accepted the good-natured jibes tossed my way. But then Father Noonan became serious.

"Say," he said, "has anyone seen Chief Dan around? I don't believe he's been down to a meal."

"Maybe he's waiting to be invited," I suggested, recalling that closed door. "I'll go get him."

"An invitation from you he won't be able to resist," Father Noonan assured me, his eyes twinkling. I wrinkled my nose at him as I sped from the room, then up the stairs to our second floor rooms.

But when I reached that closed door and put my hand up to knock, I hesitated. I didn't know the man. Maybe he didn't want to be disturbed. My knock was timid. There was no response. I started to leave, almost relieved he hadn't answered. Then something stopped me.

"Coward!" I berated myself. "Who could hear that weak-kneed tap?" And I rapped soundly.

The door opened and I found myself staring into the sombre eyes of a man not much taller than I. The whitestof hair cascaded to his shoulders, framing a face that was stern, yet somehow kindly. The angular features were softened by the years, a man certainly in his seventies. I swallowed hard, but no words came.

"Yes?" Just one word, but even in that one word his voice was so resonant. There was power and depth. I liked him.

"Won't you come and have lunch with us?" I asked.

A smile lit up his face, a smile so radiant I felt its warmth. "Thank you," he said. "I would like that."

When I finished my lunch I rose to leave, thinking Chief Dan might want to stay longer and chat with the priests. He'd spoken only briefly during lunch, only in answer to questions put directly to him. Perhaps my presence had acted as a deterrent. But when I stood he pushed back his chair and stood too. He bowed slightly to those remaining at the table and followed me from the room.

We walked down the hall together. He smiled at me and I returned the smile, wondering if I should offer to show him around. Sister Ruth Ann, hurrying down the hall, solved my problem.

"I'm glad I found you," she said. "Could you help me get the children into their costumes? We're having a dress rehearsal."

"Can do," I told her, then to Chief Dan, "Would you like to watch?"

"I would enjoy that," he said.

I helped Sister Ruth Ann get the children dressed, then joined Chief Dan on the davenport in the playroom. These children loved play-acting. They were good. Chief Dan smiled and nodded, pleased with what he saw. When they were finished they crowded around us, shyly demanding approval. Curious fingers threaded our hair. Mine had always fascinated them, fair and curly, in decided contrast to their straight black bobs. I didn't mind when they ran their fingers through my hair, but would Chief Dan? He seemed not to, smiling and nodding, patting a head.

"I have thirty-seven grandchildren," he said.

I laughed. "Thirty-seven! I have only three."

He laughed too, then admitted, "I think I would like to rest now. I will go to my room."

He stood, but he didn't leave. Instead he looked at me so I dislodged a couple of youngsters from my lap and walked with him to his room.

I paused outside his door. "Would you like me to come for you at supper time?"

"Yes, thank you," he said.

So it was I accompanied Chief Dan George to all his meals and to many other functions. He waited, always, to be asked. Though he talked little I found him delightful, becoming increasingly fond of this quiet, unassuming man. We listened to many speeches. The priests spoke of the history of Christie. I'd taken Christie more or less for granted during the years I'd been coming here. Now each poignant word tore at my heart. How could such a beautiful undertaking come to an end? Thoughts of the cove flashed through my mind. Could those beautiful times end too?

I had known Chief Dan would be speaking, but he hadn't said when and I hadn't asked. When his name was announced it caught me by surprise. What a different man he was when called upon to speak; no longer shy and reserved. He stood erect, proud. His voice was rich and full of authority, with a vibrant quality that enthralled and held the listener. The young people would miss Christie, but they must work hard at the new school, he told them. "Remember you are Indians. Be proud you are Indian. Do not forget your culture." For a moment there was complete silence, the audience mesmerized by the power of his speech. Then it came, thunderous applause. Tears came to my eyes. He saw them when he returned to his seat beside me. Smiling, he reached over and touched my hand, so gently, like a whisper of the wind.

Three days had become as one, and suddenly it was over. It ended with graduation exercises of the eighth graders, Chief Dan posing with them for pictures. And finally a High Mass, celebrated by Bishop Remi De Roo of Victoria, assisted by former Oblate missionaries; fifteen of them lined up on either side of the altar. It was impressive. It was beautiful, and when it was over we filed out silently, still caught up in the spell.

But then came the good-byes. I managed a few minutes with Rose and Alban and my Lena Bethine. Activities had precluded any real time together. All too soon, bags were packed, sleeping bags rolled up. Guests departed in droves and soon there were no more trollers bobbing at anchor in the bay.

I had decided to stay on another week before going on up coast to the cove. Several of the priests were staying and so was Chief Dan. I wondered what was in store for the old place. To desert it seemed shameful. I wandered up to my room. With a sigh I closed the door, wondering again what the future held for me at my own beloved cove. My thoughts ran in circles, getting me nowhere. A knock at the door brought me to with a start. It was Father Lobsinger.

"Hey, there! Aren't you coming down to supper? Chief Dan's waiting to be asked. And don't look so glum. We're not locking the joint and throwing the key away. We haven't made any hard and fast decisions yet, but we'll use this place in some way to further our work with the coast people. Put on a smile now and come down."

Later that evening we all gathered in the big old kitchen. Father Gerry had his guitar, as usual. Chief Dan also had a guitar. It didn't take long to get things going, and now I saw another Chief Dan. He loved to sing. He loved strumming his guitar. He and Father Gerry harmonized, the rest of us joining in.

I'd thought Chief Dan might tire and leave us, but at two in the morning his eyes still sparkled and his smile was as bright as any in the room. Perhaps it was those countless cups of coffee provided by Mary Hays who should have been exhausted after her three-day siege in the kitchen, but somehow wasn't. The songfest was repeated on successive nights. Nothing was over. There would be changes here at Christie, but Christie would continue to function.

I knocked on Chief Dan's door, one last time.

"You are leaving now?" he asked.

"Yes."

He took me into his embrace. One kiss, firm yet gentle. I would never forget.

CHAPTER 20

Wedding

Florence Michael could hardly have picked a stormier day for a wedding. My invitation had come, not from Rose and Alban, but from the groom's parents, as had previous wedding invitations I had received. So I had concluded it was the custom of my Indian friends. I'd made a hurried trip from Seattle to Tofino. In the small Catholic Church in Opitsat, across the channel from Tofino, Florence would become the bride of George Frank, and Opitsat would be her new home.

It seemed strange to be arriving in Tofino and not proceeding on to Christie. The Sisters had bought a house in Tofino where I was now staying, and were continuing their teaching at the new school. It was working out fine, Sister Laura told me, but I couldn't help thinking back to all those happy times at old Christie, and I couldn't hide the longing I felt.

"This is no day to be sad," she reminded me.

Indeed, a persistent rain falling from dismal skies had failed to dampen spirits, despite news that the time set for the Amchitka nuclear blast in Alaska coincided with the 2 P.M. wedding ceremony in Opitsat. For days Vancouver newspapers had warned that the blast might be followed by an earthquake and a resultant tidal wave. The

1964 earthquake and the tidal wave that had swept down the coast was still vivid in everyone's mind. Still, there was no thought of delaying the wedding.

"Are you concerned about the Amchitka blast?" I asked the village hairdresser.

"Some," she admitted. "A lot of the villagers have their cars packed ready to take off the moment a tidal wave is on the way." She shrugged. "Me? I'm staying. I haven't time to think about it anyway. Wait until you seethe hairstyles I've created for the bride and the brides-maids. Guess I'm as excited about this wedding as they are."

In the early afternoon we headed across the waters to Opitsat. Brother Cav was at the helm. We were met on the Opitsat side by a squadron of seagulls huddled on the beach, their heads tucked in, the grey of their wings blending with the grey of the day.

The procession to the church, though wet, was lively. Ushers held umbrellas over the girls as they ran, giggling, holding up their gowns so they wouldn't trail in the mud. Someone's washing hung on a line, a soggy assortment flapping in the wind, a bit of colour in the otherwise grey landscape. The church was packed, everyone squeezing into the smallest possible space. If there was discomfort it was all forgotten as the groom took his place at the altar.

His trousers were of royal blue velvet. A matching robe with the family insignia emblazoned across the back swung from his shoulders. He carried himself proudly. His father, Shorty Frank, was Chief of Opitsat. He would be the new Chief. Father Mac and Father O'Connor wore similar robes, embellished with colourful tribal emblems. Father Mac's was a royal blue with a sunburst design, Father O'Connor's a bright red.

Someone nudged me. "George's mother sew them all," she said.

"Did she make Florence's gown too?" I asked.

"Yes. She makes all the gowns. She sews better than anybody."

Up the aisle came the lovely bridesmaids in their lavender gowns, followed by the bride on the arm of her beaming father. Florence's gown was also of royal blue velvet and a tiny jewelled crown sparkled in her upswept black hair. She walked slowly, flashing smiles at her delighted subjects. She would be their new queen.

After the wedding ceremony we gathered at the community hall for the wedding feast. There were many speeches. Alban, in his excitement, forgot a part of his. "Excuse me," he said. "My French is not so good." This produced a roar of laughter and a round of applause. But mixed in with all the talk and the laughter there was speculation.

"If the tidal wave comes do you think it will reach Opitsat?" someone asked.

"Don't worry," someone advised. "If it comes, we will do like we did when the Good Friday tidal wave came."

That wave had made a shambles of the Indian settlement at Hot Springs Cove. Only two of the eighteen homes were left standing after the wave swept on. The church had been bounced fifty feet off its moorings. Yet they recalled it all with laughter.

They joked about one of the women who, when the water crept into her house, grabbed up old clothes and flung them on the floor.

"Someone help me mop up this water," she had cried.

"You think you can mop up the ocean?" her husband had asked her. "Come on. We go out in the boat."

So, as that first wave hit the village they had all taken to their boats, obeying a traditional command: *When the big wave strikes the only safety is far out at sea.* The elders assisted the very old and the very young. Not one life was lost. Now, here at Opitsat, though the Amchitka blast was on everyone's mind, there was no thought of leaving. The festivities went on as planned.

After the feast we all trooped into the main room of the hall for the tribal ceremony. First came the acceptance of the bride by the groom's family and the presentation of the gifts. In the time of the potlatches the gifts had been personal possessions. With the banning of the potlatches the gifts became money. Each member of the bride's family, right down to the most distant relative present, would receive an amount dictated by rank and age.

The bride, flanked by her family, marched to the centre of the room where they were met by the groom and his family. Florence's parents presented her to the groom's parents who, in turn, presented her to the groom. A table and two chairs were set up in the middle of the room. Then, to the beat of the drums, we formed a slow shuffling procession that led us to the table where we bowed to the bride, then to the groom, as we presented our gaily wrapped packages.

The procession ended and the young couple disappeared, reappearing shortly in native costume, complete with a thunderbird headdress. The headdress, carved from cedar, was heavy and cumbersome. I wasn't surprised that the marriage ceremonial dance consisted mostly of restrained stomps and carefully executed turns.

The measured beat of the drums increased in tempo. Florence and George made their exit and other dancers took their place. Many were barefoot. Some wore cedar bark or grass skirts, similar in appearance to those worn in the Hawaiian Islands. To chants and the wild beat of the drums the hours passed in a whirl of colour as the dancers executed the most demanding of dances, whirling, leaping, muscles rippling. It was beautiful. It strained the imagination.

"How can they go on and on?" I asked the young Indian girl sitting beside me. I had almost to shout to be heard. "I'm exhausted just watching."

"Is hard work," she told me. "They learn when they are just little. Practice all the time."

Finally one of the elders held up his hand for silence.

"No tidal wave yet," he said. "We think now it will not come. We give you our Survival Dance."

The dancers whirled faster than in any preceding dance. We stomped our feet in accord and shouted approval. And then it was all over. We were out in the black wet night, tromping the long muddy trail to the dock.

The wind and the waves buffeted our boat. "Hang on," Father O'Connor advised us as we neared Tofino. "It's going to be a rough landing."

Our boat slammed hard against the dock, but someone was quick with the ropes and soon had us safely snugged in. We climbed out, still buoyed by the excitement of the day, and cheerfully made our way to our separate destinations. This was my shortest visit to the coast, but certainly one of the most dramatic. Even with Christie's doors closed it had been a special time.

CHAPTER 21

Disaster and Recovery

In May I received two letters, one from Mickey McMann and one from Crystal Schoppel. Both informed me that my old log house had been broken into and ransacked.

"You'd better not plan to bring the kids up until you've had a look yourself," Crystal wrote. "I hate to be the one to tell you, but whoever broke in was pretty thorough. The place is a shambles. You can stay here in Tahsis with us and Johnny will run you out." I stared at the letter, unbelieving.

"Grandma, why would anyone want to do that to us?" Jeff asked.

"I don't know, Jeff. It had to be someone we don't know."

"What will we do, Grandma?" Pam asked. "Where can we go?"

It had become, I realized, as unthinkable for them to spend a summer in the city as it was for me.

When I went out with Johnny Schoppel to ascertain the extent of the damage, shambles didn't adequately describe what we found. I could understand robbery, but to destroy or mutilate what they didn't want was vicious beyond my comprehension. Why did they have to batter all three doors? And my clothes strewn all over the house, my own special rocker smashed through the floor! Even the stove was gone. Could they really have needed a little old wood stove? Why? Why?

But it was the pictures that tore at my heart . . . ripped from albums, tossed on the floor and walked on. Suddenly, bitterly, I hated those who had done this to me. It was as if they had violated my very person. That was me lying there on the floor, kicked and shoved aside. How dare they? How DARE they? Tears stung my eyes.

"Go ahead, cry!" Johnny urged. "I want to. Looks like a bunch of damn pigs was rootin' round in here. What I'd gve to get my hands on the bastards!"

I managed to speak. "I could clean up the mess, I guess." But as I walked through the house, determining the extent of my losses, I knew it was hopeless. Bedding, linens, dishes, silver, pots and pans, all the essentials of housekeeping gone.

Johnny raved on. "Damned buggers were sure methodical. Mickey just happened in and caught them at the tail end of their spree. Whole damn family working. Kids too. Had everything packed in boxes and were carrying them down to their boat. Mickey told them to put the stuff back, then took off to Tahsis to report it to the R.C.M.P. The hell those bums put it back!"

He paused but when there was no response from me, continued his tirade. "I wonder how many trips they made in that boat before Mickey caught them? Plenty, I'd say, from the look of things. They'd rented or borrowed that boat, we found out later. Some damn trucker! Came in over the new road. Took off damn fast too, once Mickey was on to him."

I spoke then, but with little hope. "I could replace some of what's been taken, I suppose."

Johnny shook his head. "With the road open there'll

be more of their kind in. Unless you were to be here the year round it would happen again."

He was right, of course. I remembered how hard it had been for Wally and me to bring in all we needed. Alone I couldn't do it, and even if I could it would be futile. The road was open. Nothing would be safe, not my home, not my possessions, possibly not even myself. Johnny was sorry. But sorrow couldn't begin to describe a hopelessness so intense it blocked out even anger, leaving nothing but apathy.

"I'm sorry," Johnny murmured again.

How many times I'd heard those exact words! I'd heard it from George when I came up on the *Uchuck*. And I heard it from Harold, one of the crew.

"I could kill the bums," he'd said. "The old house was always a place you could go to if you were in trouble. Hell, I've visited you myself. I got caught in a blow out in my little putt-putt on one of my days off, and I knew you'd want me to come in."

Yes, the old house had sheltered so many. I stood, irresolute, wanting to run, wanting to stay. Dear God, how I wanted to stay.

Johnny sensed my feelings. "Come on," he said. "Let's get out of here. There's nothing you can do. No sense tearing yourself apart. I hurt too, you know."

"I know, Johnny. Go on down to the boat. I'll be along in a minute."

Reluctant, he nevertheless did as I asked. I walked from room to room, saying a special good-bye to each. I ran my hands along the cedar paneliing in the upstairs bedrooms, caressed the old log walls in the living room and the hanging waste basket Wally had made for me my first birthday here at the cove. How much easier, I thought, to accept a natural disaster than one perpetrated by people. One *can* forgive nature. I walked to the door.

It hung open, a window broken. And then I heard a familiar rustle in the bushes.

"Minniebelle. Oh, Minniebelle!" She emerged from the bushes, her head cocked to the side, regarding me placidly as she had so many times through the years. "Oh, Minniebelle, I'll miss you so. Don't ever go away, ever, ever!"

"Mrs. Flynn," Johnny called from the boat. "You okay?"

"I'm coming," I answered, squeezing back the tears as I ran down those steps to the beach perhaps for the last time.

"I'm sorry." Mickey said when Johnny and I stopped in at Esperanza on our way to Tahsis. "If you want to bring the kids up, you can stay here, you know.'

"I'm sorry," Crystal said, putting her arms around me as I walked in the door of their home in Tahsis. "You're always more than welcome to stay here."

"I'm sorry, Mom," Dirk said later. "I heard you were here with Johnny and Crystal. I'd like to sit out there with a shotgun and blast whoever comes in. That was home to me too, sorta. Look, I've got to make a run to Gold River tomorrow. Ride along on the tug with me. Huh?"

It was a slow, slow trip. The tug seemed to just mosey along. But I was in no hurry to leave behind this country I loved so much. I feasted my eyes on the blue of the meandering channels, on the intense green of the mountains. And I was in no hurry to leave Dirk. His youth and confidence were a tonic.

"Don't worry, Mom. I bought me a place on Texada Island. It's beautiful too. You can always come there."

So I had a number of options. What would be best for the kids? When I got back to Seattle there was a letter waiting from Father Mac.

"We heard what happened," he wrote. "A darn shame, but why don't you and the kids come here to Christie this summer? We're having a series of summer retreats for Indian and white families. Plenty of room for you and your tribe too."

I'd long wished the kids could visit Christie. Now was the time. And they loved it, as had so many children before them. They roamed the sandy beach, dared the breakers, climbed the cliffs. They explored the old building, fascinated by the number of rooms, by rooms within rooms, by cubbyholes under the stairs. They hiked back through the evergreens to a lake where they swam and played in the blue waters.

"It's fun, Grandma," Jeff admitted. "I like it here," and then added wistfully, "but I sure do miss the cove. I guess it's the nicest place in the whole world."

His words triggered a longing I'd tried to suppress. It was hard to hold back the tears. I loved Christie. I always would, but there was just no place like home.

That night as we were preparing for bed in our mini-apartment, a knock came at the door. I was surprised. It was late. Everyone should be in bed, I thought, as I hurried to the door.

Gilbert John stood on the other side of the door. He and his family had an apartment for the summer over the carpenter shop. Gilbert was a couple of years older than Greg. He had two brothers and a sister. My three had become best friends with the Johns, but it was rather late now for a social call. I was about to tell him so but he spoke first.

"Our dog got a bone stuck in her throat," he said. "We can't get it out. Us kids, Mum too, try to hold her so Dad can get it out. She fights us all the time. We can't hold her. We want you to get it out."

I stared at him for a moment. Five of them couldn't

hold her yet they expected me to remove the bone. "Okay," I said at last. 'I'll see what I can do."

As we walked across the yard to the carpenter shop I looked up at the stars brightening our way. Dear God, *what* can I do? I had helped Wally remove any number of bones, but we'd had a clamp to hold the mouth open. We could give an anesthetic if necessary. We'd had proper instruments. I had nothing now but my bare hands. Still, these people believed I could do it. I had to try.

The dog, a terrier mix, had hardly calmed down during the short time it had taken Gilbert to come for me. Isaw the fear in her eyes. She couldn't understand or rid herself of the discomfort, no matter how she pawed at her mouth. She regarded us all with suspicion, evading an outstretched hand. A small dog with a more complex nervous system could be harder to control than a larger animal.

"Katari," I said to Gilbert's mother. "Let's have a coffee and give her a chance to calm down."

Before too long I was able to pick her up. I made no attempt to touch her mouth. Instead I patted her gently, scratched behind her ears, talked in soothing tones, and when I felt she was ready I turned to Mr. John. "Take her and hold her with her front legs between your fingers." We sat on the floor. "Leonard, take the back legs and lay her on her side. Gilbert, you hold her mouth open and don't let it shut no matter what. I can't afford to lose a hand."

Gilbert nodded, proud of his responsibility. I quickly spotted the bone. It was not in her throat, but wedged between two of her back teeth at the roof of her mouth.

Working gently with a table knife I could wiggle the bone, but couldn't free it. I asked Katari for some tweezers. The bone came away easily. The Johns released their hold and the little dog bounced to her feet, frisking around us, happy again. I felt good as I walked back under the stars to my own apartment.

I opened the door to the apartment quietly and tiptoed in, sure all three of my grandchildren would be asleep, but a soft voice came in the darkness.

"Did you get the bone out, Grandma?"

"Yes, Jeff, I did."

"Good. Now I can sleep."

All three loved animals but with Jeff there seemed to be a special bond, as if he understood their ways, their joys, their hurts. I smiled as I reached down and patted his head.

Still, when we returned to Seattle, I couldn't put the cove out of my mind. I'd been determined I wouldn't be bitter over my loss, but determination had not erased the hurt, the aching and longing that sometimes seemed more than I could bear. On one particularly gloomy day a letter came from Father Gerry. I slowly turned it over in my hands, reluctant to open it. Father Gerry was always so confoundedly cheerful, and I was in no mood to be cheered.

"Well, that old house of yours is still doing a job," he wrote. "Three Indian lads from Queens Cove were out in their boat when the gas engine exploded. Luckily, they were close in and able to swim to shore. They were badly burned though, one especially. The weather was miserable, cold and blustery. In their condition, if they hadn't been able to get to that house of yours, they'd have died for sure. Alban came in three days later to check on the old place, found the boys and took them to hospital at Esperanza. We all thought they'd drowned, but I'm happy to report they're doing okay."

I sat for a long time, just holding that letter in my hand. And from it, gradually, a warmth seemed to spread through my body. The old house was not finished. It was still there, offering refuge to anyone who might need it. And it was here ... in my heart. No matter what the future held, no matter whether we could go back, or whether we couldn't. For Maureen, for Greg and Pam and Jeff, and especially for me, that house and the cove would forever be a part of us. Something that time could not erase, something that no one could ever take from us.

Epilogue

The years have seen many changes. My grandchildren are now in their twenties. But one thing has not changed: our love for the cove and for old Christie School at Kakawis. We have made visits to the cove though we have been unable to live there as before. My youngest grandson, Jeff, has suggested we buy a boat we can live in during our stays at the cove, storing it at Esperanza when it is not in use.

I have also made many return trips to Kakawis. When Christie School closed in 1971, the Oblates offered the facilities to the west coast Indians to be used for something constructive and beneficial. Meetings were held with the native people from Kyuquot to Ucluelet. Many ideas were considered, then abandoned, until Dick Leo suggested a rehabilitation centre. Since alcohol is a distressing problem, and because the entire family is usually affected, it was decided to make it a family centre.

Many people were involved in this new project but the two core people responsible for the program were Father James MacDonell and Sister Lorraine La Marre. For five years they laboured to serve their Indian clients. Families stayed for a six-week period. There were daily counsel-

FLYNN'S COVE

ling sessions, group therapy and individual instruction. Pre-school and lower-grade children were supervised and taught by Sisters of St. Ann, who spent varying periods of time at Kakawis. The older children were ferried daily to the mainland to attend school at Tofino or Ucluelet. When the families returned to their homes, there were follow-up visits by the Oblates and Sisters. I, also, have had the opportunity to visit with some of these families. The program has made a difference.

When Father MacDonnell and Sister La Marre left, Father Gerry Guillet assumed the responsibilities. Then on July 15th, 1983, disaster struck. The old school burned to the ground. The fire started on the third floor, which had been closed off, and the cause of the fire is un-determined. A program which had achieved beneficial results, however, could not be abandoned.

The Oblates purchased sixteen trailer units which were renovated and converted into six family units. Also purchased was a large unit to be used as a dining, class, and meeting room. These buildings were placed on a new site at Kakawis as the old school site is being reserved for more permanent buildings.

The Provincial Government, which partially funds the operation, agreed to continue their support despite a three-month delay before operations could be resumed in November. Which all proves that if the spirit and the will is there, people will get things done.